Y0-BDY-021

BACKGROUND TO ARCHAEOLOGY

Britain in its European setting

Desmond Collins
Ruth Whitehouse
Martin Henig
David Whitehouse

Cambridge
at the University Press
1973

0823768

Published by the Syndics of the Cambridge University Press
Bentley House, 200 Euston Road, London NW1 2DB
American Branch: 32 East 57th Street, New York, N.Y. 10022

Cambridge University Press 1973

Library of Congress Catalogue Card Number: 72-95408

ISBNS:
0 521 20155 1 hard cover
0 521 09808 4 paperback

First published by The Association for Cultural Exchange,
Cambridge, 1970
Revised edition 1973

Printed by offset in Great Britain
by Alden & Mowbray Ltd
at the Alden Press, Oxford

Contents

68699

0823768

Acknowledgements

We are grateful to the following for permission to reproduce illustrations: Almqvist & Wiksell Förlag AB, Ch. 4 Fig. 2a-d from N. Åberg *The Anglo-Saxons in England* (1923); John Baker Ltd, Ch. 1 Figs. 2, 4, 7 from J. Wymer *Lower Palaeolithic Archaeology* (1968); The British Museum, Ch. 4 Fig. 3a; Cambridge Antiquarian Society, Ch. 4 Fig. 2e-g from T. C. Lethbridge *A Cemetery at Lackford, Suffolk* (1951); The Clarendon Press, Oxford, Ch. 3 Fig. 5 from R. G. Collingwood and R. P. Wright *The Roman Inscriptions of Britain Vol. 1* (1965); Edinburgh University Press, Ch. 2 Figs. 6a, 7a, 7b, 10 redrawn from S. Piggott *Ancient Europe* (1965); Methuen & Co. Ltd, Ch. 2 Fig. 2a from E. C. Curwen *The Archeology of Sussex* (1937), Ch. 2 Figs. 6b, 8 redrawn from V. G. Childe *The Dawn of European Civilisation* (6th edn. 1957), Ch. 3 Figs. 2, 10 from R. G. Collingwood and I. A. Richmond *The Archaeology of Roman Britain* (1969); Max Parish Ltd, Ch. 3 Fig. 3 from G. C. Boon *Roman Silchester* (1957); Penguin Books Ltd, Ch. 3 Fig. 11 from A. Boëthius and J. B. Ward-Perkins *Etruscan and Roman Architecture* (1970); The Royal Norwegian Embassy, London, Ch. 4 Fig. 7; The Society of Antiquaries of London, Ch. 3 Fig. 6a-b from B. Cunliffe *Excavations at Fishbourne 1961–1969 Vol. 2* (1971), Ch. 3 Fig. 8 from R. E. M. & T. V. Wheeler *Verulamium. A Belgic and two Roman Cities* (1936); Thames and Hudson Ltd, Ch. 2 Fig. 3c from J. F. S. Stone *Wessex* (1958), Ch. 2 Fig. 6c from H. N. Savory *Spain and Portugal* (1968), Ch. 2 Fig. 6d from L. Barfield *Northern Italy* (1971), Ch. 4 Fig. 6 from J. Beckwith *Early Medieval Art* (1964); Weidenfeld and Nicolson Ltd, Ch. 1 Figs. 8, 9, 11, 12, 13, 14 from F. Bordes *The Old Stone Age* (1968).

Ch. 3 Fig. 4 drawing by Trevor Stubley.

Foreword

The picture of the past presented by archaeological research changes rapidly as work proceeds. New surveys of the changing pattern are constantly necessary, and on this score *Background to Archaeology* needs no apology. But it is also the product of a specific set of circumstances, and has a well-defined aim, to help those with an interest in the archaeology of this country to appreciate the wider context which helped shape the development of Britain.

The book grew out of the annual *Archaeology in Britain* seminars for American students arranged by the Association for Cultural Exchange, and the authors have been involved in the running of these seminars over several years. The views and interpretations offered here are those of able young professional archaeologists who have considerable experience of the needs of people with an intelligent interest in the subject but little specialist knowledge.

Having initially been published in a small edition by the Association for Cultural Exchange, *Background to Archaeology* is now being made available to a wider public in a revised edition. In the belief that this work can be of use to a large audience, I am happy to take this opportunity of wishing well to the venture.

J. D. Evans
*Professor of Prehistoric
Archaeology
University of London*

NOTE ON DATING

Most of the dates quoted in chapters 1 and 2 are derived from radiocarbon analysis (C14). Recent work on the calibration of the C14 time scale by dendrochronology (tree-ring analysis) has shown that radiocarbon dates diverge from dates in calendar years by varying amounts at different periods. The maximum divergence recorded, in the fifth millennium B.C., is c. 800–900 years, but the precise calibration has been calculated only from c. 4500 B.C. In chapter 2 the dates have been corrected where possible (from c. 5000 B.C.), but to avoid confusion and because it is not possible as yet to correct earlier dates (including of course all those quoted in chapter 1), throughout chapter 2 the dates derived from C14 analysis are quoted in parentheses after the corrected dates, prefaced by the letters C14. For dates before 5000 B.C. the letters C14 alone are quoted in parentheses afterwards, as a reminder that they are uncorrected. Dates after 5000 B.C. which are derived from the historical calendars of Sumer or Egypt are of course quoted as such, as are dates derived from C14 after c. 1200 B.C., when they appear to be sufficiently accurate for the broad chronological brackets employed in this account. To summarise, dates labelled with the letters C14 represent radiocarbon years: those unlabelled are thought on present evidence to represent actual calendar years.

1
Early Man

Desmond Collins

Man's remote ancestors left their marine environment for dry land some 350 million years ago. Subsequently they lived a shrew-like existence, but about 50 million years ago they were outmanoeuvred by the true rodents and took to the trees of the then continent-wide rainforests.

Some anthropologists doubt whether our direct ancestors ever lived in the trees, but others do not believe we could have acquired the stereoscopic colour vision, delicate grasping function and remarkable sight and motion co-ordination which we share with higher primates, without an arboreal phase. Man differs primarily from other higher primates (the apes and monkeys) in his upright posture and adaptation to relatively treeless country. His arboreal phase probably ended during the rapid expansion of the savanna some time after 40 million years ago.

The first specifically human feature to appear in the fossil record is the reduction of the dagger-like interlocking canines characteristic of other primates (replaced by small canines no longer than the incisors and facilitating side to side mastication). *Ramapithecus* from deposits of 8 to 15 million years' antiquity in Kenya and India certainly had reduced canines. How could our ancestors have managed without them, when for apes the long canines are essential in breaking open hard fruits and other food as well as in fighting and menacing? Perhaps as Pilbeam has suggested a certain level of tool using had already become part of *Ramapithecus'* pattern of behaviour, and clubs were used for defence and sharp stones for cutting. Moreover a connection is probable between having hands free for tool use and an upright walking posture, which only the hominids have.

'Australopithecus'

The first good evidence of upright posture comes with the earliest substantial sample of hominid skeletal material – that of *Australopithecus* from the Transvaal, South Africa. The pelvis of

Australopithecus in particular attests to our kind of stance, and is unlike that of an ape. A number of different hypotheses have been offered to explain the evolutionary position of this hominid and human evolution in general.

They include the view that only one species of man existed at a time and that the fossil hominids of the last few million years (including *Australopithecus*) are representative of a single but very varied evolving population: this is the 'continuity' hypothesis. At the

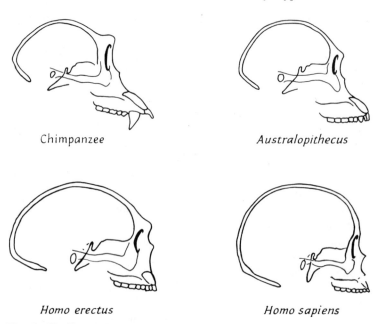

Chimpanzee   Australopithecus

Homo erectus   Homo sapiens

Fig. 1. Skulls of the three main stages of human evolution compared with Chimpanzee.

other end of the spectrum, is the view that *Australopithecus*, along with other man-like fossils, belongs to a line distinct from modern man. Some have gone so far as to find him a place among the apes, or at least quite distinct from man's evolution: this is the 'extinction' hypothesis of fossil man. Increased knowledge of *Australopithecus*, especially his human-type teeth and posture, has largely eliminated the theory of ape affinities.

There are many variations on these views, as well as a compromise position very nearly intermediate between the two. The most important variation on the continuity theory is that there were two contemporary species of *Australopithecus*, the hominid genus

2

known from over five million years ago down to under one million years ago, who was small brained (under 900 c.c.) and big toothed. The larger and more robust species on this view (perhaps a vegetarian according to Robinson) ultimately became extinct. The more slender species *Australopithecus africanus* was a partly carnivorous toolmaker who evolved into later men. Consistently with this sort of view *A. africanus* could be included in the genus *Homo*. Another popular candidate for a side branch, as we shall see, is Neanderthal man.

Of the variations on the extinction theory, those which nominate a few fossils as true human ancestors are particularly characteristic. A well-known example is the view offered in 1964 by Leakey that some hominid fragments from Olduvai ($1\frac{1}{2}$–2 million years old) should be called *Homo habilis* and should be regarded as the true ancestor of man, contemporary with *Australopithecus* who should be regarded as a non-ancestor. An important conference held in 1962 to consider the conflict between extinctionist and continuity interpretations came out in favour of a modified continuity theory and proposed three main stages of human evolution: *Australopithecus (africanus); Homo erectus; H. sapiens* (fig. 1). Two recent accounts of these controversies are Pilbeam (1970) and Napier (1971), and they present the arguments for both sides of the *habilis* debate.

Toolmaking and hunting

Man's present-day survival would be impossible without his technology, and tools have played a vital part in his rise to mastery of the material world. Following an idea of Benjamin Franklin, Oakley has suggested that we equate the beginning of man with the beginning of undoubted toolmaking. It is not always quite clear what should rank as toolmaking, and it might be objected that sporadic toolmaking would precede more regular forms. At the same time we have evidence that already nearly two million years ago man relied to a considerable extent on game for his survival: i.e. he was a hunter. Meat does form a minute proportion of the diet of some primates like baboons but is untypical of the diet of the primate world. Man however, having lost the potentially useful dagger-like canines, could clearly not have indulged in regular carnivorism without tools for cutting up the game. Hunting and toolmaking are thus linked, since the means of killing and dismembering the food are provided by the piercing and cutting tools. Such tools would have been of little value while the vegetivorous adaptation lasted.

Assuming we are right to equate toolmaking with meat-eating, we

3

may now ask when this important advance was made. A key site for our understanding of this is Olduvai Gorge in Tanzania, lying between the Serengeti game park and the Great Rift Valley. Exposed in this twenty mile long gorge is the best sequence of deposits in the whole of Africa for the crucial period of the Pleistocene – the last two million years or so in which the ice ages fall.

In Bed I, the older part of the sequence, both the main types of early hominid have been found – Olduvai hominid 5, a well preserved skull of the robust or vegetivorous type, and fragments of several individuals of the slender type (*habilis* of Leakey). They are all dated to about $1\frac{3}{4}$ million years ago by the potassium–argon method. From levels nearly 2 million years old onwards, flaked stone tools undoubtedly made by man are found, often on old land surfaces covered by fresh falls of volcanic dust, and in situations where all possibility of natural fracture can be excluded. Two other East African sites in Kenya and Ethiopia, but both close to Lake Rudolf, have yielded stone tools dated between 2 and 3 million years ago. In the same area fossils of *Australopithecus* now go back to $3\frac{1}{2}$ million years ago at Omo and about $5\frac{1}{2}$ million years ago at Lothagan, but at the time of writing no tools earlier than 3 million years ago are known. In spite of the considerable differences of opinion on the age of the earliest stone tools in Asia and Europe, it now seems likely that toolmaking is over one million years older in Africa than elsewhere, and this is accordingly the likely homeland of man.

Simplicity and lack of variety of well defined types characterise the tools of Bed I at Olduvai, which are called Oldowan after this site. The most characteristic type, called a chopping tool (fig. 2) is a quartzite or lava cobble flaked in two directions to produce a sharp edge. Their use is not known except for the probability that they were necessary for carnivorism. The remains of small game on the same floor – lizards, crabs, juvenile pigs etc. – may be the remnants of a typical meal. A ring of piled stones may have been a windbreak or simple dwelling.

Oldowan tools are still found in Bed II at Olduvai perhaps about a million years in age. Both Bed II and contemporary northwest African sites have tool assemblages including new types and a little greater variety. A multifaceted spheroid (fig. 3) in particular became popular, perhaps for tenderising meat or for throwing. At least half a million years ago a significant change had occurred. Big game – elephants, rhinos, giant sheep etc. – are found on the living floors, and one of the commonest tools of stone age man, sometimes called

4

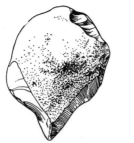

Fig. 2

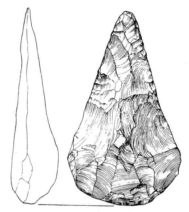

Fig. 3   Fig. 4

Fig. 2. Chopping tool ($\times\frac{1}{2}$).
Fig. 3. Faceted spheroid ($\times\frac{1}{2}$).
Fig. 4. Handaxe ($\times\frac{1}{2}$).

a handaxe (fig. 4), for want of a better name, is found with the kills. The early meat-eating hunters may have served a long apprenticeship in catching small and juvenile creatures, supplemented perhaps by a bit of scavenging, but by half a million years ago they had become proficient as big game hunters, an important step in man's mastery of his fellow creatures.

'Homo erectus' and his culture

We have skulls of the time span 900 to 300 thousand years ago from Java, China (near Peking and again near Lantian), Algeria, and Olduvai itself (hominid 9). Less certainly, jaw and other fragments are known from Transvaal, Israel, from near Heidelberg and from near Budapest. At the 1962 conference a number of scholars agreed to group these as *Homo erectus*. They indicate an overall increase in brain size compared to *Australopithecus africanus*, for all exceed 750 c.c., which is often regarded as the crucial lower limit for modern type intelligence. The range is from 775 to 1,225 c.c., but is based only on a small number of accurately measured skulls. Teeth are smaller than in *Australopithecus*, the face is reduced in size, but the skull is thicker and the stature greater.

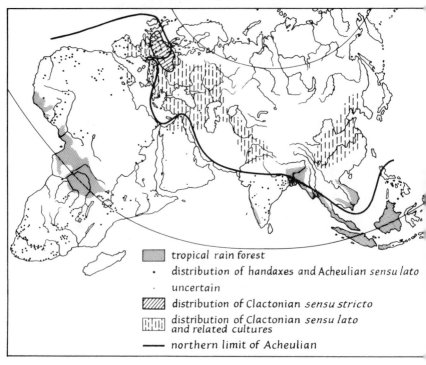

Fig. 5. Distribution of Acheulian and Clactonian, in the wider sense of these terms; after Collins (1969).

The man of this new evolutionary stage was still physically distinct from modern races. The average brain size (near 1,000 c.c.) was well below that of modern men (around 1,350 c.c.) The teeth were larger, the face heavier and the skull thicker; but most of these people were already bigger than modern pygmies. Much of this can be explained by regarding *Homo erectus* as a giant version of *Australopithecus africanus* with selective reduction of the teeth and face. He is also the obvious ancestor of *Homo sapiens*.

Larger body size and perhaps the acquisition of an efficient spear would have aided big game hunting, and this in turn would have helped man to colonise new environments in Eurasia. It seems logical to equate such improved hunting proficiency and technology with the emergence of *Homo erectus,* a larger bodied and presumably more subtly brained hominid, ancestral to our own species. The advent of new tools has already been mentioned and one very significant development following the Oldowan was the emergence of at least two contemporary traditions of toolmaking. These are geographically distinct, but both probably have local variants. They are the Acheulian, with handaxes as its most widespread trait (fig. 5); and the Clactonian, best known in northern Europe, but with related cultures across Eurasia. The Clactonian has a different set of characteristics, some such as chopping tools not unlike the Oldowan, others more original like the biconical core and related flaking method (fig. 6), and the distinctive Clactonian notch.

Another achievement of this period seems to be fire, traces of which were found with Peking man, at Vértesszöllös near Budapest and at Torralba in central Spain. At this latter site no human remains have yet been found, but finely preserved elephant slaughter sites were revealed. The scattered traces of charcoal and burnt bones from Peking man's lair in the Choukoutien limestone fissures are suggestive (but not conclusive proof) of fire-using. The apparent absence of hearths before about 150 thousand years ago may indicate a long period when fire was known, but could only be produced with great difficulty or gained from natural fires or even borrowed from other communities, as is supposed to have been the case with the Andaman islanders in the Bay of Bengal. The necessity for fire arose no doubt from the penetration into new and cooler territories when winter nights became too cold for survival without the aid of artificial warmth; skins would also have helped. The fact that some of the human bones from Choukoutien were broken, and allegedly charred has been used to suggest that Peking man was a cannibal. Evidence that they preyed on animal game is slight at Choukoutien, but the pips of the hackberry were found and this suggests a vegetable element in their diet.

Of the social organisation of *Homo erectus* and his predecessors we can say nothing from direct evidence. Comparison can perhaps most profitably be made with surviving primitive hunters who are generally monogamous and organised in small bands of perhaps twenty to fifty persons. Prior to toolmaking and hunting a structure more like that of the baboon troop may have been more likely, with

7

large numbers in the troop, usually over fifty, and with a hierarchy based on strength among the males and no permanent male–female bonds. Such a rough and tumble society may have disappeared but it is suggested that many instincts survive from such a 'subhuman' stage or earlier. For example eating, breathing, temperature control etc. go back at least to our mammal origins over 100 million years ago.

Recently there has been much interest in the possibility of an innate aggression which we share with much of the animal world, though without sharing the built-in checks to its exercise. This inheritance has long since ceased to be necessary as a defence against predators, as we are now the world's most successful predators: nor is it performing a second original function of maintaining an adequate territory or social space for each of us, since at the advent of large community life (if not before) all spacing mechanisms broke down. Probably the 'community neurosis' found today in overcrowded settlements is such a mechanism, but we contrive at the moment with the aid of culture to prevent it fulfilling this function. Aggression has probably been favoured in historical times as it confers a slight competitive advantage in the acquisition of mates and the breeding of offspring: we recognise it increasingly today in the form of social and economic competition, which we ambiguously deplore and practise.

The time-scale

Although a clearer picture of the climatic fluctuations of the Pleistocene is rapidly emerging, there are still grave difficulties in reconstructing their time-scale. Most archaeologists concerned with the Pleistocene hunting peoples (or Palaeolithic period as they have called it for over a hundred years) think that the archaeological record should be considered in its geological context: the nineteenth-century concept of archaeological 'epochs' (*Acheulian, Mousterian, Magdalenian* etc) is taken seriously by few modern workers. Probably the best established fact about the last geological period (the 2-million-year-long Pleistocene) is that there was an alternation of warmer and colder climate, affecting it seems the whole planet.

The colder periods, provoking massive extensions of continental ice like that of Greenland, are often called glacials and the warmer periods interglacials. More universally the glacials have low sea levels, and the interglacial seas return to the present levels or higher. This glacial terminology is of course far from satisfactory for Africa, where glaciation is confined to the mountain peaks, and elsewhere a glacial period was characterised by climate which is warm by European standards. The further one goes back, the less clear is the evidence for details of climatic change, but even so indications of quite severe temperature lowering go back to 2 and even 3 million years ago; over 5 million years ago however, temperatures seem to have been universally warmer. Thus in the time of *Australopithecus*, fluctuations in temperature, and perhaps more importantly in rainfall, were an important factor in the changing environment. Indeed they may have provided the stimulus in response to which man began to move in his own characteristic evolutionary direction.

The present temperate period (Flandrian) began about 8300 B.C. (C14) and the cold period before it usually called Würm or Weichselian about 75,000 B.C. Before this the last interglacial (called Ipswichian in England but more usually Eemian in Europe) probably began about 100,000 B.C. The date of the interglacial before this (Hoxnian in England, Holstein in northern Europe) is more difficult to fix. Some put it as recent as 130–170,000 B.C., others around 200–250,000 B.C., yet others nearer one million years. The intermediate figure seems to be the most likely, and high stands of the sea at this time are recorded as far apart as Morocco and Alaska. There are at least two earlier interglacials, the Cromerian and Tiglian, perhaps about half a million and one million years respectively, but the sequence of events becomes more obscure at this time.

Man in Britain
The first advent of man to Britain is naturally of particular interest to those working in British archaeology. A large number of claims have been made over the last eighty years for the presence of man at a very remote time, most notably on the basis of alleged artefacts from the East Anglian crags (pre-Cromerian marine deposits) and the Kentish plateau. Present opinion tends to reject these claims and it must be admitted that none of these crude specimens (often called eoliths) resemble the well established artefacts now known from other parts of the world at the same time, for example at Olduvai.

There are two other main reasons why eoliths must be regarded as dubious. First because many are found in deep water deposits where man could not have lived. Secondly the kind of stone tools one would expect are piercing or cutting tools with some kind of sharp edge, but eoliths have steep blunted edges such as are produced by crushing, and it is generally assumed that they were made by natural

9

action. They are made on frost split pebbles and are blunter than most normal unworked stones.

Setting aside the eoliths and other dubious claims, we find that evidence of man begins reliably in the Hoxnian/Holstein interglacial, and this time horizon is thus of importance. Before this interglacial was a period of very extensive ice advance (called the Lowestoft (= Mindel) advance) down to the Thames valley. Not surprisingly such a period supported little or no life and man was clearly a newcomer to Britain after it. The Hoxnian is a period of much human activity in Britain and our only important fossil skull – from Swanscombe – is of this time. In modern classifications this is also the first skull included in *Homo sapiens,* the surviving species.

The temperate periods are most reliably recognised by their vegetational sequences. These have often been recovered by analyses of the pollen which fell at different levels in the accumulation of organic muds, peats etc., which are characteristic of interglacial periods in northern Europe. Stone tools have been found in two such localities, at Clacton in Essex and at Hoxne in Suffolk (type site of the Hoxnian). The stone tools from Clacton include many thick flakes, some chopping tools and other types which, following a suggestion by Warren, have come to be called Clactonian (see pp. 6–7). The tools from Hoxne are Acheulian. Both these occupations date from near the middle of the Hoxnian/Holstein interglacial.

In spite of the importance of these two sites, we have in fact learned more from Swanscombe. Pollen evidence is still inadequate; but several other types of evidence can be used to correlate the high terrace river gravels of Barnfield pit with the Hoxnian: notably molluscs (shelled animals), mammalian remains, erratics, river gradient and stratigraphy. Above all, however, rich assemblages of Clactonian from the lower series and of Acheulian from the middle and upper strata strengthen the link with the Hoxnian. Such a situation implies that in Britain the Acheulian follows the Clactonian, and confirmation of this is found at other sites like Barnham in Suffolk. Thus there are two possibilities: either the Acheulians are a new population who move in and replace the Clactonians; or the Acheulians are the same people as the Clactonians, who are latterly making a new set of tools. Since the Acheulian style of toolmaking was established well before the Holstein, on the second hypothesis the Clactonians 'reinvented' it. But is it really likely that they would reinvent so accurately such a distinctive technology, while so many feasible alternatives remained untried?

Accordingly I incline to the view that the Clactonian and Acheulian are of different origin, the former perhaps primarily Eurasiatic, the latter African and Iberian in background. The Clactonians lived at the time of the dense forests of the first half of the Holstein, while the Acheulian occupation corresponds to the time when the forests were thinning and open country was presumably supporting more large mammals, which would well suit a hunting population. Whether the Clactonians were herd game hunters is less sure, but as the first to colonise the temperate forests, they would find a range of foods such as nuts and root plants, in addition to possibilities like river fishing, and the catching of fowl and other birds and small woodland vertebrates.

Swanscombe man

The Swanscombe skull, found with Acheulian tools, has been the subject of much dispute. The accounts following the discovery of two pieces in 1935 and 1936 stressed that it differed little or not at all from modern man. However, most fossil skulls differ from present-day man in the frontal, facial and jaw bones, all lacking in Swanscombe. A second skull of about the same age from Steinheim in Germany has the facial and frontal portions, albeit in rather crushed condition.

Interpretation of the evolutionary position of Swanscombe man (or rather woman) is closely connected with the interpretation of the Neanderthals who are a mere 50,000 years old and are the last fossil population which differs importantly from modern man. Those who follow the extinction hypothesis tend to hold that all Neanderthals died out without issue, and are in no way connected with modern man's evolution: they tend to include Steinheim and even Mauer (the lower jaw from near Heidelberg) in this separate 'doomed' line. According to Vallois (1954), the main exponent of this view, Swanscombe is the sole representative at this time of our ancestors. An intermediate view regards Swanscombe and Steinheim as the same population, ancestral to both the Neanderthals and to our own line. Finally the continuity hypothesis sees three successive stages: Swanscombe–Steinheim, Neanderthal, and post-Neanderthal or Crômagnon.

A key point in testing these notions is the similarity of the surviving Swanscombe fragments to Steinheim on the one hand, and to modern man on the other, but the similarity of Swanscombe to some Neanderthals is also interesting. Exhaustive metrical and statistical comparisons by Campbell (in Washburn 1963 and Ovey

11

1964) found the two Holstein age skulls more similar to each other than to any others, with a Neanderthal from Mt Carmel next in similarity. Even on the surviving bones Swanscombe was outside the range of a normal sample of modern man, in particular in the skull bone thickness which exceeds that of the Neanderthals. The extinction hypothesis and an early separation of the Swanscombe and Steinheim lines are thus most improbable. With estimated cranial capacities of 1,170 c.c. and about 1,270–1,300 c.c. for the German and English skulls respectively, an average brain size smaller than that of present-day Europeans is indicated. This, coupled with the larger facial structure, is the most obvious difference.

Little is known of the habitations of Swanscombe man and his predecessors. Several successive dwelling places were found by de Lumley at the Terra Amata site close to Nice (de Lumley 1969). They were probably surrounded by temporary wind breaks of branches supported on posts, the holes of which survive. Hearths had been protected from the prevailing wind by small stone walls, which would not have been neccessary in a permanent, draught-proof dwelling. Terra Amata may have been occupied before Swanscombe, but a living area found at Stoke Newington in north London is closer in age. Here a nineteenth-century antiquary, Worthington Smith, found two pointed stakes of birch, four feet long, which had supported branches of *Clematis* matted with fern. Numerous burnt stones indicate a community with fire as well as wind breaks to protect them from the cold.

Penultimate glacial
The treeless or tundra zone north of the temperate forests was apparently not occupied before the Holstein. The first evidence for man cohabiting with the animals of the tundra, mammoth, woolly rhino, giant elk etc., is from the (penultimate) glacial following the Holstein, sometimes called Riss or Saale. This evidence is from north European sites like Baker's Hole at Swanscombe, the adjacent Ebbsfleet channel, and Markkleeberg near Leipzig. Archaeologically the phase is recognisable by the rapid increase in a style of flaking (called Levallois), which involved primary preparation of the core so that the flake finally removed had a shape determined by the preparatory working (fig. 7).

The Riss glacial also witnessed the development of new tool types (in the Charentian tradition which probably derives from the Clactonian tradition) notably a thick steeply retouched D-shaped tool grouped with the so-called sidescrapers or *racloirs* (fig. 8). If these were indeed sidescrapers for the preparation of skins (a point not easily demonstrated at the moment), they too may represent an adaptation to cold climate. Certainly one may speculate that survival at night when man moved into first the cool temperate latitudes and later the tundra latitudes would have been impossible without some protection: skin cloaks, easily obtained from the animals hunted, would have been ideal.

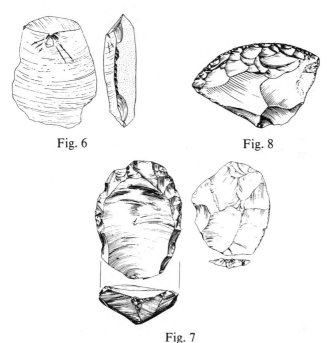

Fig. 6   Fig. 8

Fig. 7

Fig. 6. Clactonian flake ($\times\frac{1}{2}$).
Fig. 7. Levallois core and flake ($\times\frac{1}{2}$).
Fig. 8. Mousterian Quina racloir *(or side scraper)* ($\times\frac{1}{2}$).

Intensive cave occupation spanning all seasons of the year and thick hearths indicating long burning fires are typical of the last glacial period. Sometimes the caves are close together and all the indications point to a thorough exploitation of some particular food resource, presumably herd game. Cave occupation certainly begins as early as late Riss times, and hearths are found in sites like la Baume Bonne in south-east France (de Lumley 1969–71). Cave

13

occupation and hearths may go back a little earlier but this is not yet satisfactorily documented. Probably it was the sophisticated control of fire which made cave dwelling possible, and initiated the rich way of life associated with their occupation.

Neanderthal man and his culture

It is convenient to refer to fossil man of the period 100–c. 35,000 B.C. (Eem interglacial and first half of the Würm) as Neanderthal man, but the wide range of variation makes this a very questionable procedure. The culture of the period 75–35,000 B.C. (early Würm) is often called Mousterian on equally slender grounds, mainly because of the contrast with what follows it. In reality the Mousterian is a complex of different types of assemblage (Bordes 1968), some of which can be traced back to earlier traditions, notably the Acheulian and Charentian (which is an extension of the Clactonian). This complex represents a period of intensive cave occupation.

Because the people of the Charentian buried their dead, the best known Neanderthals (la Chapelle, la Ferrassie etc.) are of this tradition. There are no Neanderthals associated with the Acheulian of this time except very fragmentary and dubiously dated finds like those from the Cotte de St Brelade on Jersey, the only British finds. Non-Charentian skulls (e.g. Saccopastore in Rome and Gibraltar) tend to differ from the better known types, as do Asiatic and African skulls of the period (Mt Carmel, Solo, Broken Hill etc.). But all have brow ridges, low foreheads, receding chins and heavy facial architecture. Where do the Neanderthals fit into human evolution? This is one of the most controverted questions in Palaeolithic studies.

The most popular view over the last fifty years as pointed out by Brace (1967) has been that Neanderthal man died out without issue. He was replaced by the 'tall and fair' Crômagnons with 'lofty brows, prominent chins, superior mentality and physique'. After a struggle in which the 'the cunning, degraded, but cowardly' Neanderthals are overcome by the 'noble and virile' Crômagnons, the world is inherited by our ancestors. Presented in this way, it reads like Siegfried and the Nibelungen – except that Siegfried survives. Adherents of this view have never found any clear evidence for our type of man developing contemporarily with the Neanderthals in any major region of the world, nor have they offered any reason why he should have done. Worse, such a view takes no account of the physical and cultural survivals from the Neanderthal period.

The Neanderthal extinction hypothesis (which is a classic example of hominid extinction hypotheses in general) has appealed mainly for the following reasons: because at first sight Neanderthals looked too different to have evolved into post-Neanderthals (a group poorly represented in the fossil record); because there did not seem to be enough time; and because nobody could conceive how it might have happened. This hardly absolves us from looking for an evolutionary explanation. Brace believes that the continuing process of reduction of the masticatory apparatus and hence the face suffices to explain such an evolution.

A rather subtle variant on the evolutionary view is based on a process called neoteny, which refers to the prolongation of juvenile features into adult life (de Beer 1950). There is a wide belief that the process was crucial in the evolution of the first vertebrates and again in the evolution of mammals. An analogous process has certainly happened in human evolution, most obviously in prolonging the period of immaturity and growth. The precise mechanics of the process are not fully understood, but it is probably controlled by secretion from the pituitary gland, and will usually lengthen the period during which juvenile morphology lasts, while advancing the point at which sexual maturity is reached to an earlier stage in physical development.

Any evolutionary explanation of the disappearance of Neanderthal features (sometimes called gerontomorphic) and the transition to modern (paedomorphic) form must posit advantages achieved by the transition. For the neoteny hypothesis one might suggest a number of advantages. The juvenile form has a relatively larger frontal lobe to the brain (emphasising what is probably the most crucial area for human brainwork). Again juvenile apes are more intelligent or at least better able to learn than older apes. The long youth period in humans is essential to our culture, which involves much learning, and its lengthening is part of neoteny.

Probably the most important reason why it would be at the end of the Neanderthal phase that such a change would take place is related to the exceptionally large Neanderthal brain (16–1700 c.c.) of the time range 40–60,000 B.C. If Neanderthal mothers had the same size pelvic apertures as those of today, then childbirth would have been exceedingly difficult, and there would have been a very high mortality rate in birth – the most immediate of all forms of natural selection. Neoteny, in slowing pre-natal size increase, would lead to birth at a time when head and brain size were much smaller, and would be a kind of escape mechanism. Finally one might speculate that sexual selection would favour neoteny, for if our preferences are not entirely new, Neanderthal women without brow ridges would find it easier to get and keep mates than those in whom they were large.

Neanderthal man's achievements are interesting. His exploitation of the hunting resources of certain favoured areas such as the Perigord and the Mediterranean Levant (Lebanon, Israel etc.) was very successful, leaving a testimony of cave deposits crammed with artefacts and game remains. The burials at la Ferrassie and other sites indicate some advance over the previously rather casual attitude to the dead; but at the same time there is a high infant mortality rate (implied by four or five infants with two adults) of perhaps 70 per cent. Long graves had been dug for extended burial, the man and woman were head to head. Over one child lay a slab of limestone, on which were pairs of small cup marks or carved hollows. Associated with the Acheulian tradition on the other hand we find evidence of the use of ochre and even simple 'crayons' carved from pieces of limonite and manganese. Culturally Neanderthal man seems to foreshadow much that we note as developing in the post-Neanderthal period.

Crômagnon man and the Leptolithic

Over the deposits of the Mousterian (for which the name Middle Palaeolithic is sometimes used) lie deposits often called Upper Palaeolithic, or to use a more convenient term Leptolithic. These follow on from the end of the Mousterian around 35,000 B.C. down to about 10,000 B.C. when occupation of caves became rare at the close of the Würm glaciation. The sample of fossil man in Europe from this new period (very meagre until its latest part) can be called Crômagnon man, after some skeletons from a cave in the centre of the rich cave occupation area of south-west France. Crômagnon man differs little from modern Europeans.

In the Mousterian, flakes of varying breadth predominate, but these are progressively replaced by longer and thinner 'blades' and more importantly by 'specialised' tools like the burin (fig. 9) (probably a bone carving chisel) and a variety of projectile or spear points, with blunting or pressure flaking to give them their characteristic shapes (figs. 10, 11). In addition the first standardised bone tools are found, notably the split based, and bevel based points and later barbed harpoons (figs. 13, 14, 15). The term Leptolithic for this new level of refined stone technology is in some ways preferable to Upper Palaeolithic (which perpetuates outdated epochal notions, and has for some writers racist overtones of a conquering superior race, as well as confusing both these ideas with

16

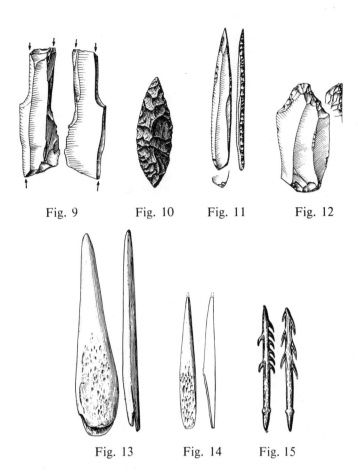

Fig. 9   Fig. 10   Fig. 11   Fig. 12

Fig. 13   Fig. 14   Fig. 15

Fig. 9. Burin ($\times\frac{1}{2}$).
Fig. 10. Foliate (leaf point) ($\times\frac{1}{2}$).
Fig. 11. Gravette point ($\times\frac{1}{2}$).
Fig. 12. Grattoir (end scraper) nosed type ($\times\frac{1}{2}$).
Fig. 13. Split based bone point ($\times\frac{1}{2}$).
Fig. 14. Bevel based bone point ($\times\frac{1}{2}$).
Fig. 15. Barbed harpoons ($\times\frac{1}{3}$).

a technological definition). Like the Mousterian the Leptolithic has a number of variants or cultures. Those in south-west France and some elsewhere have been dated by C14.

As research has proceeded the sequence of events in the Leptolithic of certain favoured parts of south-west France has turned

17

out to be very complex. In 1872 de Mortillet envisioned only two or three stages, but by 1912 Breuil's sequence had at least twelve. This ended with the Magdalenian (six stages): in the middle came the Solutrean (with three stages and its chief tool the foliate or leaf point (fig. 10)), and at the beginning the Aurignacian with three stages. In place of Breuil's three evolving stages we now recognise at least ten stages in this early part, and at least two traditions – Perigordian and Aurignacian. Running from about 35–18,000 B.C., these include: Perigordian I, Aurignacian I–IV, Perigordian IV, de Noailles, Perigordian VI; Protomagdalenian, Aurignacian V and Protosolutrean. Most of these are of limited distribution.

Cave man in Britain

The evidence of cave occupation in Britain during the last glaciation is slight. Mousterian tools are found in outlying caves like those of Creswell Crags in northern England, of Coygan in south Wales and elsewhere in the west. The site of Oldbury in Kent is the richest Mousterian in England, and was probably a rock shelter. It belongs to the Acheulian tradition, as apparently do other assemblages rich enough for diagnosis. Open sites, with a type of handaxe characteristic of the early Mousterian, are found in the lowest terrace deposits of rivers in south and east England, as at Little Paxton on the Ouse and at Christchurch near the mouth of the Avon in Dorset.

Nearly fifty years ago Garrod (1926) presented the British Leptolithic in terms of the sequence of south-west France. A foliate from the north Welsh cave of Ffynnon Beuno, for example, was ascribed to the Solutrean, and a 'busked' burin was attributed to the Aurignacian. The foliate actually resembles Polish and German examples which belong to the more recently recognised Szeletian. Likewise backed blades from Gough's cave in Cheddar Gorge have been attributed to the Upper Aurignacian (Perigordian IV of present classification). In reality they compare better with tools from the close of the Magdalenian and following Azilian, or nearer at hand to the late Würm Tjongerian cultures of Holland and Belgium. The regional difference was partly recognised in the adoption of the name Creswellian, but this was coupled with the dubious view that the local tradition lasted from the Perigordian IV (about 24,000 B.C.) for over 10,000 years until the end of the Leptolithic. More likely the Creswellian represents a late colonisation of northerly regions about 10,000 B.C. when the intense glacial conditions finally ameliorated at the end of the Magdalenian.

If the Creswellian is no earlier than the close of the classic

18

Leptolithic sequence, what is contemporary with the rest of this sequence in Britain is reduced to a handful of sites with rarely more than a dozen typical tools: Pin Hole and Robin Hood's cave at Creswell and Kent's Cavern in Devon are perhaps the best examples. Such a situation should probably be interpreted in terms of occasional visits during milder phases during the glaciation, most notably the 'Paudorf' interstadial about 30–25,000 B.C. Recent C14 dates for Kent's Cavern confirm this view. Culturally all the tools could be attributed to a late Szeletian, though some of the foliates resemble the Font Robert point, a type found in the southwest French sequence about 25,000 B.C. Paviland cave has yielded a skeleton of Crômagnon type, and recently a C14 date, perhaps too recent, of about 16,000 B.C.

The earliest art

Cave art is perhaps the greatest achievement of the Leptolithic. The earliest representational art is found in the Aurignacian I stage (overlying the Perigordian I which has only ochre) especially in the Vézère valley, which flows into the Dordogne and ultimately the Garonne. The amount and variety of this art dating back perhaps to 32,000 B.C. do not allow us to doubt its genuineness or importance: it includes outline animal engravings and simple non-perspective paintings such as the crude aurochs's head from Castanet shelter – perhaps the earliest extant art piece. The horns stick up in a wide V shape, while the head is in side view. The red or black paint has probably been smeared on with the fingers. In the Spanish cave of Covalanas, red deer and horse have been shown in outline, painted with the fingers since much of the outline consists of fingerprint size blobs.

Sex symbolism is particularly characteristic of Aurignacian art. Commmonest is a vulvar symbol – pear shaped at first, and subtriangular in a later stage (perhaps 29–26,000 B.C.). The earliest examples of the female statuettes called Venuses, notably from Willendorf in Austria (fig. 16) and Petřkovice in Czechoslovakia are contemporary with this later Aurignacian. Significantly they have the same shaped vulva representation as is found in contemporary south-west France, indicating that art styles were very widespread. Other symbolism from the Vézère valley includes phalluses, notably one carved out of bison horn, and numerous cup marks, sometimes arranged in circles.

Venuses characterise the next stage of art in western Europe which is associated with the de Noailles culture about 25–21,000 B.C.

Besides the stone venus of Tursac and the exquisite ivory venus of Lespugue, other fine art is found in the de Noailles culture. We have painted and engraved animals and fine engraved human figures on a stone plaque. Although an improvement in fineness of line is found in the Aurignacian IV engravings from the Ferrassie rock shelter, de Noailles engraving can be distinguished by a further overall improvement. Obviously connected with the venus statuettes are the well known limestone bas reliefs from Laussel, such as the woman holding a horn.

Fig. 16. Willendorf venus ($\times$ c. $\frac{1}{2}$).

It is hard to find distinctive characteristics in the art of the Solutrean phase and those phases immediately before and after it. Superb large scale bas reliefs were, however, made in the late Solutrean at Roc de Sers and other sites. Some workers believe that these are stylistically like Lascaux, the most famous of the painted caves, whose dating is not entirely clear. The cave was occupied, however, in early Magdalenian times, about 15,000 B.C. judging from one radiocarbon date.

The late Leptolithic and its art
Both from the wealth of small art objects found in Magdalenian

strata, and from the general consensus of opinion on the dating of the major decorated caves, such as Altamira, Combarelles, Niaux, Font de Gaume and Gabillou, it is clear that the Magdalenian represents the climax of artistic activity (especially between about 14 and 11,000 B.C.). Among the small objects, decorated weighted heads of spear throwers are particularly important and perforated batons (fig. 18) were also often decorated. Small disc buttons, perhaps cloak fasteners were also finely engraved. The carved objects belong mainly to functional classes. In contrast to Aurignacian art other pieces of stone or bone were rarely engraved.

Fig. 17. Savignano venus $(\times\frac{1}{4})$.

In the field of cave mural art, more than one colour on each animal is typical of Lascaux, Altamira and Font de Gaume; previously one colour only was used. It seems that a brush or perhaps a fur pad was used in Magdalenian painting: previously it had been applied with the fingers or blown through a tube. Magdalenian bas reliefs do not differ much from those of the late Solutrean, but the Cap Blanc horse frieze and Angles female reliefs are among the most impressive sculptures of all time. The fineness of line from Teyjat and Gabillou is unsurpassed in hunting art, though slightly later engravings from Addaura in Sicily are also exceptional. The most complete illustrated account of cave art is Leroi-Gourhan (1968), but a more compact source is Ucko and Rosenfeld (1967). The most original and perceptive book is Giedion (1963).

One explanation of the motivation behind Palaeolithic art which has often been offered is hunting magic. Support for this idea comes partly from ethnographic parallels but especially from a group of sites in the Pyrenees, of which Montespan is the most important. Here a bear had been modelled in clay, probably covered with a real bear pelt, and then speared. Nearby a wall covered in soft clay had been crudely traced in the form of animals, which had then been speared repeatedly leaving the spear holes to be seen today. The nearby cave of Trois Frères has a famous painting of a man, slightly obscure in detail, but embellished with engraved animal parts, including antlers, animal ears, paws (perhaps of a bear) and a tail.

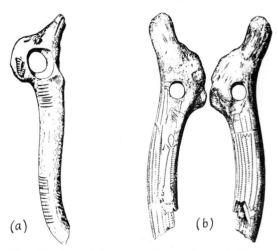

(a)

(b)

Fig. 18a. Magdalenian perforated baton ($\times \frac{1}{6}$).
Fig. 18b. Maglemosian perforated baton ($\times \frac{1}{4}$).

Besides the art and finely carved bone tools such as bone harpoons, spear throwers and spatulas, the Leptolithic from Aurignacian onwards includes a variety of musical instruments. There are whistles and flutes with as many as six fingerholes and perhaps sixteen notes. A disguised man engraved in the Trois Frères cave is either playing a bow as a musical instrument, or according to others blowing a flute. One can only speculate on any myths or heroic tales that may have existed at this time, but it is hard to deny that the cultural level is not very different from that of dawning civilisations. It is tempting to equate this whole new level of culture with the emergence of cerebrally modern man.

One may well ask whether the later Leptolithic shows any real advance over the earlier stages. Certainly the passing of 25,000 years would allow time for newly evolved modern man, who was probably already Caucasoid in Europe, to build up a store of culture in the form of traditions, religious observances etc. As the new tool kits were elaborated, the archaeological record shows a greater variety of material culture. An invention which may have been very significant was the barbed harpoon or spear point. In France this appears in Magdalenian IV (about 12–13,000 B.C.). Not much later, perhaps 11–12,000 B.C., it is found in the north German reindeer hunters' camp of Meiendorf. Subsequently the barbed projectile head seems to have become widely spread: it is found in central and eastern Europe, western Asia, the Nile valley, sub-Saharan Africa, Australia and Siberia. With the Magdalenian harpoons are found antler spear throwers (which may well have existed in wood earlier).

The spear thrower is good indirect evidence that the bow was not used. The earliest good evidence of the bow dates from about 8500 B.C. at Stellmoor in north Germany, where a hoard of arrows was found. Later, bows themselves are found, as at Holmegaard in Denmark. There is a tendency for bows to be associated with a small worked flint blade (the obliquely blunted point, sometimes tanged), and a host of small blade armatures or barbs called microliths (figs. 19, 20, 21, 22). The latest Magdalenians who had some microliths may also have had the bow. The use of the bow (like the barbed harpoon and spear thrower) probably represented a major advance in hunting efficiency, and it too has spread very widely, usually in reciprocal distribution to the spear thrower and blowpipe.

The Flandrian
After the end of the Würm, about 8300 B.C., hunting culture lasts some four thousand years in western Europe – rather less in eastern Europe and western Asia, and rather longer in places where the arrival of farming was slow, such as north-westernmost Europe and Sub-saharan Africa. This prolongation of hunting culture in the Flandrian period, sometimes called Mesolithic, does not seem to contribute any essential cultural advance. Clearly the main revolution which overthrew the Leptolithic way of life was farming; and there is no obvious reason why late Würmian culture was not sufficiently advanced to achieve domestication. In fact we now suspect that the Neolithic (or food producing) Revolution had already been largely accomplished by the beginning of the Flandrian in northern Iraq and maybe in Turkey and the Jordan Valley as well. Here the Leptolithic had already ended before the end of the Würm.

There is an overall tendency to miniaturisation of stone tools

23

already apparent at the end of the Würm. Indeed one should remember that microlithic blades were characteristic of an Italian culture contemporary with the Magdalenian. In areas formerly characterised by open plains the advent of the forests of Flandrian times provoked the invention of equipment to deal with it – notably axes. As far as areas like south-west France and the middle Danube are concerned, a sharp fall in population seems likely to have been the main adaptation attendant upon the decimation of the herd faunas.

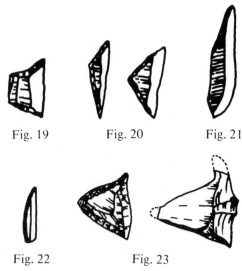

Fig. 19   Fig. 20   Fig. 21

Fig. 22   Fig. 23

Fig. 19. Chisel tip arrowhead (×1).
Fig. 20. Triangles (×1).
Fig. 21. Oblique point (×1).
Fig. 22. Dorsal (backed) point (×½).
Fig. 23. Petit tranchet *derivative arrowheads (P.T.D.)., neolithic type derived from chisel form* (×1).

Some of the most detailed evidence of the adaptations of hunting culture in Europe comes naturally enough from its latest stages. Much archaeological evidence comes from lake and bog sites which have been preserved by the accumulation of peat and organic mud. Such a site is Star Carr in east Yorkshire (Clark 1954). Here a lakeside platform of felled birch branches had supported a small community of deer hunters around 7500 B.C. when open birch woodland was beginning to give way to pinewoods. One birch tree had been felled and laid from the platform into the lake as a kind of pier. A paddle among the many organic finds preserved presumably indicates some kind of boat, and dugout canoes have been found in contemporary Holland. Red deer and roe deer, however, made up three-quarters of the food bones with elk, wild ox and boar also significant. This is also the earliest site where domesticated dog has been found.

Numerous barbed bone points were found, but whether they were used in hunting or fishing is not known. Some deer frontals, with the antlers still on them but hollowed out for lightness, were clearly worn as head-dresses, but whether for disguise in hunting or magically cannot be easily decided. Pieces of iron pyrites for striking sparks and tinder collected by drying fungi indicate how fire was made. Rolls of birch bark were also kept, perhaps for their resin. Certainly small flint armatures were secured in shafts with resin and one such has been found. Most likely the flint armatured weapons were for hunting animals. There was no indication of huts or tents. For a recent discussion of this site see J. G. D. Clark's *Star Carr: a Case Study in Bioarchaeology* (1972).

From earlier times however, we do have tent-like dwellings, even in groups. Examples are Borneck in north Germany, Pincevent in northern France, Plateau Parrain in south-western France, Pavlov in Czechoslovakia, and Kostienki in Russia; all these are Würmian. In the Flandrian they are rarer: Abinger, Farnham, and Deepcar in Britain, and Retlage in Germany are examples. Without understimating the value of these discoveries, one must realise that from the surviving traces it is impossible to be sure if any of these were permanent huts, or to know if any were occupied for more than a few weeks.

The main cultures in Britain during the period 8300 to 5500 B.C. can be grouped as Maglemosian and Sauveterrian. With the arrival of dense mixed oak forest about 5500 B.C. (C14) evidence of settlement is sparser, and mainly belongs to the so-called Horsham culture, which combined Maglemosian and Sauveterrian tool types with a form reminiscent of the continental Tardenoisian. Although a few such hunting groups may have been present when the earliest farmers arrived, there is little or no evidence for their later survival. Indeed the features in the early farming cultures of Britain which have an origin in hunting culture, such as the *petit tranchet* derivative arrow head (fig. 23) are specifically continental types. At the time of the arrival of the first farmers in Britain, the cultural heritage in the country was virtually extinct.

2

From the Beginnings of Farming to the Spread of Civilisation

Ruth Whitehouse

When Gordon Childe was searching for an objective criterion of progress, applicable to archaeological data, he chose the simple biological definition of population increase. Anything that allows the expansion of population is by this definition aiding the evolution of the species and therefore advantageous (Childe 1936, 4th ed. 1965: 9–14). If we wish to employ a criterion not confined exclusively to physical development, we may take the expansion of cultural choices available to man. Anything that increases the range of choices or, in other words, enlarges the scope of man's activities, can be regarded as advantageous. This has the virtue of being a specifically human criterion, applicable to mental and, if one likes, spiritual as well as physical development, but is none the less amenable to objective assessment and is free of any subjective ethical judgement.

It is the object of this book to chart in outline the course of human progress, defined in these non-ethical terms, from the origins of man to the end of the medieval period in the Old World, especially those parts of it particularly relevant to Britain. In chapter 1, which covered by far the longest part of the human story, we saw how man gradually increased his control over the environment and in consequence increased his range of cultural activities. Individually significant contributions to this cultural evolution include the beginnings of toolmaking, probably linked with the development of hunting, and the control of fire, but the gradual improvements in lithic and other technology, with which the archaeologist is so largely concerned, also contributed to the increasing control exercised by early man over his environment. In chapter 2 I shall be dealing with later phases of human progress, which took place at a greatly accelerated pace, and the various developments responsible for this. As in the earlier periods, these include both individual discoveries and inventions of 'revolutionary' significance in themselves, and gradual improvements in technology.

The origins of farming

Judged by either of the criteria discussed above, one of the most significant advances in the whole of human evolution was the change from a hunting and gathering to a food-producing economy. This allowed man far greater control over his environment, led directly to a rapid population expansion and, with the increased availability and security of the food supply, created both the time and the opportunity for a greatly enlarged range of cultural activities.

It is currently fashionable to criticise the use of the term 'revolution' to describe this change, as it has become clear that the whole development took a considerable period of time, that it took place in several different areas and that it took several different forms. However, I think it is useful to retain the term, since no other word conveys the momentous and indeed revolutionary effect the change, *once fully accomplished,* had on the course of human evolution.

The beginnings of food-production

The end-product of the food-producing revolution was settled village farming, based on a combination of agriculture and stock-breeding. The paths towards this end were several and various, but there seem to have been some shared preconditions. Firstly, it is clear that the domestication of wild plants and animals could only have taken place within the zone where the wild prototypes of the domesticates occurred. The crucial combination seems to have been of the grasses – emmer wheat and barley – and sheep and goat, since it was on this combination that the first viable farming economies were based. Other domesticated plants were of secondary importance and other animals – cattle and swine – were domesticated appreciably later. Allowing for the present distributions reflecting inaccurately the original pattern, we find that the wild ancestors of the crucial domesticated plants and animals occur in a wide area of the Near East, running east from the Mediterranean coast to the Zagros mountains and northwards from the Red Sea and the Persian Gulf to Anatolia. Another precondition for the development of food-production may have been the changing climatic conditions at the end of the Pleistocene. In the zone in which we are interested here this took the form of increasing aridity, which would have restricted the availability of wild foods. This might have led hunting and gathering communities to concentrate on particular plants or animals, which would have preluded their actual domestication. An alternative and quite opposite view holds that a precondition to the food-producing revolution was a 'broad-spectrum' diet, in which almost anything was regarded as potential food – an attitude to diet which would have favoured experimentation and innovation and may thus have provided the basis for the development of farming (see papers by Braidwood and Flannery in Ucko and Dimbleby 1969). Be that as it may, the domestication of plants and animals took place in at least three distinct areas of the Near East within the period c. 10,000–6000 B.C. (C14). The three areas are:

(1) *The Zagros mountains and adjoining plains.* In this area domesticated sheep are recorded as early as c. 9000 B.C. at Zawi Chemi Shanidar, where they accompanied hunting and the harvesting of cereals, probably wild. Further south at Ali Kosh, c. 7500–6750 B.C. (C14) there were domesticated goats and a few sheep, emmer wheat and a little einkorn and naked two-row barley combined with the collection of wild plant foods, hunting and fishing. By c. 6000 B.C. (C14) sheep and goat were still the only domesticated animals in the south, but pigs were apparently in the process of being domesticated c. 6500 B.C. (C14) at Jarmo, further north. After c. 6000 B.C. (C14) leguminous crops were grown in addition to wheat and barley throughout the zone.

(2) *The Levant.* In Syria, Palestine and Jordan a parallel development can be traced. c. 7500 B.C. (C14) the Natufian culture was characterised by a concentration on gazelle hunting and by harvesting of wild cereals. This stage was followed at Jericho and Beidha by the Pre-pottery Neolithic A stage, c. 6800 B.C. (C14), associated with emmer wheat and hulled two-row barley. By the Pre-pottery Neolithic B stage at Jericho, einkorn and leguminous crops had been added to the plant repertoire, while at Beidha there was emmer wheat and barley of a type very close to the wild prototype. At at least one site, Tell Ramad, the fauna consisted exclusively of wild animals, but at Jericho and Beidha goats *may* have been bred.

(3) *Southern Anatolia.* Nothing is known about the earliest phases of food-production in this area, but by c. 7000 B.C. (C14) there was a culture at Haçilar associated with naked six-row barley, emmer wheat, lentils and other pulses, accompanied by hunting of wild

0823769

28

animals, but probably not domesticated animals. By 6000 B.C. (C14) there was a well developed farming culture at Çatal Hüyük, based on cultivated emmer, einkorn and bread wheats, barley, peas, vetch and lentils and domesticated sheep and goat, still accompanied by hunting.

It is interesting that on present evidence only in the Zagros did the domestication of animals precede the cultivation of plants, and indeed both in Anatolia and the Levant there were at an early stage flourishing farming cultures based on agriculture without domesticated animals at all. Interesting also is the fact that while along the Zagros there were only small villages of farmers, both at Jericho in the Levant and at Çatal Hüyük in Anatolia there were much larger communities with some evidence of economic specialisation and centralised organisation – a precocious development that, as it turned out, led to nothing at this stage.

There are several indications that there were connections between the three areas: for instance the plastered floors and skull cult characteristic of the Levantine Pre-pottery Neolithic B phase are echoed at Haçilar in Anatolia and Anatolian obsidian was traded to the Palestine sites and even to Ali Kosh. However, it seems likely that the domestication of plants and animals proceeded more or less independently in all three areas.

Settled village farming

We have seen how during the seventh millennium B.C. (C14) there emerged in different areas settled village farming communities practising a mixed farming economy or plant cultivation alone, accompanied by the continuing exploitation of wild food resources. The development of these communities differed and it is clear that during an early stage societies practising some degree of plant or animal domestication had economies that were viable alternatives to those based on pure hunting and gathering, but were not at that stage noticeably superior. With the achievement of settled village farming, however, the inherent superiority of food-producing over food-gathering became apparent. This manifested itself in a number of ways:

(1) There was a rapid population expansion which by the biological definition proposed by Childe itself indicates the superiority of the new economy. There were more communities and these were larger than in earlier periods, indicating that a given area of land could support a larger number of farmers than hunter–gatherers.

29

(2) The new economy spread outside the natural habitat zone of the wild prototypes of the original domesticated plants and animals. In the course of this, adaptations were made by the domesticated species to the new environmental conditions. In addition new species were domesticated. It now seems possible that cattle were domesticated as early in Greece as in Anatolia and certainly earlier than in the Levant or the Zagros. Swine, on the other hand, may have been domesticated independently in southern Russia, and this area certainly became the home of the domesticated horse a little later. Millet may have been added to the plant repertoire in Greece or south-east Europe, and much later spelt wheat, rye and oats were domesticated or became significant crops for the first time in the north and west of Europe.

(3) There was a dramatic increase in the range of cultural activities, which I suggested earlier might be used as a second criterion of progress. There were advances in the fields of technology (for instance, pottery was invented and new lithic techniques, such as grinding and polishing of hard rocks, devised), housing (better-built dwellings accompanying permanence of settlement), trade (increased in quantity and scope) and religious life (manifested in various ways, such as animal and human figurines, wall paintings, funerary cults and construction of shrines). In fact any of these practices can occur individually or in combination in contexts other than that of settled village farming, but there is no mistaking the outburst of new cultural activity that followed the establishment of a viable farming economy and was presumably made possible by it. It seems to me that even for the sake of the fashionable argument, it is difficult to deny the revolutionary significance of the new economy, once fully established, in giving man substantially greater control over his environment and in opening up vast new cultural potentialities.

The spread of the farming economy
An important part of the history of man in the Old World after the completion of the food-producing revolution (and indeed there is a parallel situation in the New World) can be seen in terms of the spread of this form of economy almost to the furthest corners of the earth. Indeed so superior has this economy proved to that based on food-gathering that, while at the present day large parts of the world are still inhabited by peasant farmers little influenced by the industrial economies of the developed countries, only in very small isolated areas and in extremely hostile environments, such as the Kalahari desert or the circumpolar region, do tiny groups of hunter–

gatherers survive. The farming economy spread in all directions from the zone where it originated, though the development of farming in south-east Asia may have been independent of that of the Near East. Here I am concerned only with the north-western expansion into Europe.

The spread of the farming economy is well documented in the

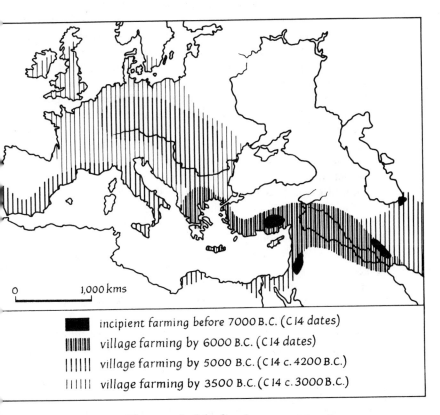

0   1,000 kms

■   incipient farming before 7000 B.C. (C14 dates)

|||||||| village farming by 6000 B.C. (C14 dates)

|||||| village farming by 5000 B.C. (C14 c. 4200 B.C.)

|||||| village farming by 3500 B.C. (C14 c. 3000 B.C.)

Fig. 1. The spread of the farming economy.

archaeological record and it is known that by c. 3500 B.C. (C14 3000 B.C.) the practice of farming had reached the northern and western extremities of temperate Europe (only with further technological developments at a later period did this economy spread beyond the temperate zone) (fig. 1). It is less clear, however, by what methods the techniques were spread: possible alternatives include large-scale movements of peoples, introducing the new economy in its entirety and bringing with them the actual domesticated plants and animals, some movements of people introducing the new techniques which were then rapidly adopted by the indigenous population and applied to local plants and animals, and finally stimulus diffusion, by which we mean that only the idea of farming was spread. In fact we can rule this last alternative out, since the presence of some plants and animals outside their natural habitat zone indicates that initially they must have been introduced by people (certainly where natural barriers such as mountain ranges or seas had to be crossed). In general the archaeological evidence for most areas of Europe indicates an almost complete cultural break between the Mesolithic and the Neolithic in each area, which would suggest that initially a fairly large-scale immigration of people was involved, introducing a fully developed culture. On the other hand, where the actual farming practice is concerned, present opinion favours the view that there was considerable local domestication of native plants and especially animals and that many of the domesticated animals were therefore not the descendants of introduced stock. In addition it is likely that indigenous Mesolithic communities rapidly adopted the techniques of farming after their introduction to any area. Thus the spread of farming must have been brought about by a combination of migration and diffusion, with the emphasis on migration in the first instance, diffusion in the later stages.

Because of the oriental origin of the farming economy, one way in which the European Neolithic can be viewed is in terms of the progressive adaptation of an oriental cycle of cultures to European conditions. Thus, moving west and north, one can see the cultures becoming progressively less oriental and more distinctively European. This adaptation to European conditions also had a chronological dimension, with later cultures being more noticeably European and less oriental in character, though new contacts with or intrusions from the east gave *some* later cultures an oriental aspect.

The farming economy spread into Europe by three main routes: (1) along the northern coasts of the Mediterranean Sea; (2) along the river Danube and its tributaries; and (3) across the north European plain. Along each of these routes a distinct cycle of cultures can be recognised. The movement of peoples and ideas from the east seems to have occurred in a series of waves, and at the eastern ends of the three routes these can often be distinguished. However, there was a tendency for the waves to catch each other up and to merge into single cultures in the northern and western parts of Europe.

Mediterranean route

The earliest farming communities in this area belong to a Pre-pottery Neolithic, which was already in existence in Greece in the seventh millennium B.C. (C14). It may have occurred also in Romania and Jugoslavia in the sixth millennium (C14), but has not been recognised further west. Little is known about this culture, which is defined chiefly by its farming economy and a few distinctive flint types.

This was followed by a group of cultures defined by the presence of Impressed Ware – coarse pottery decorated while soft with a variety of impressed designs. It may have originated in southern Turkey or northern Syria, but its main development was in Greece and further west. It was in existence in Greece by c. 6000 B.C. (C14), had reached Italy before 5000 B.C. (C14) and Iberia by c. 4800 B.C. (C14 c. 4100 B.C.). This group constituted the first farmers in the central and west Mediterranean (fig. 2a).

Probably beginning as early as Impressed Ware, but surviving to a later date was a series of cultures defined by painted pottery of various styles. This group, which has a very oriental appearance, was less widespread than Impressed Ware, occurring no further west than Sicily and Lipari, although imported pots and some other features of this group did percolate further west in small quantities.

In the western part of this zone – northern Italy, Switzerland, southern France and Iberia – and with an Atlantic extension into central and northern France and even Britain, we find a series of cultures known as Western Neolithic, defined chiefly by a group of related plain wares of simple rounded forms. The origin of this group, which was in existence in south France by c. 4750 B.C. (C14 c. 4000 B.C.) and had reached England by c. 4100 B.C. (C14 c. 3500 B.C.) has long been in doubt, but present opinion favours a derivation from Impressed Ware, which is often associated with plain wares, especially in the west Mediterranean (fig. 2b).

Danubian route

Along this route settlement was more or less confined to the rich loess soils along the valleys of the Danube and its tributaries. The cultures differed considerably from those found along the Mediterranean route, although there was some overlap in eastern Europe. Apart from the possible existence of a Pre-pottery Neolithic in the east, there were two main waves of Neolithic cultures along this route.

The first wave consisted of the Starčevo culture in the east, which is really an Impressed Ware culture with some painted ware also, associated with tell settlement (i.e. permanent settlements) and rectangular dwellings of wattle and daub. It was in existence by c. 5500 B.C. (C14). West of this area was the L.B.K. (or linear pottery) culture, formerly called Danubian I, with a distribution extending from eastern Europe almost to the Channel coast. It had reached the limits of its distribution in Germany, Holland and eastern France by

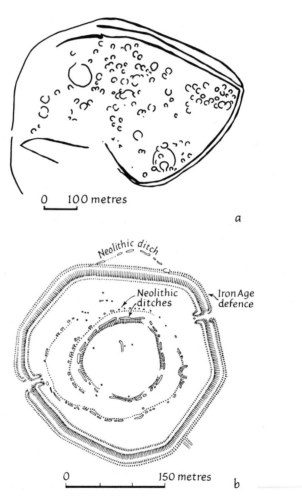

0   100 metres

a

Neolithic ditch

Neolithic ditches

Iron Age defence

0   150 metres   *b*

Fig. 2. *Neolithic settlements: (a) Passo di Corvo, southern Italy;*
(b) The Trundle, England (this site also has Iron Age defences).

34

shortly after 5000 B.C. (C14 c. 4200 B.C.). This was a remarkably uniform culture, associated with, as well as distinctive pottery and stone types, long post-built timber dwellings and possibly a cyclic system of agriculture. In both these characteristics it represents the earliest farming culture really adapted to temperate European conditions.

The second wave of cultures found along this route, e.g. Vinča, Tisza and Lengyel cultures, formerly called Danubian II, was far less uniform than the first wave. Like the painted ware groups in the Mediterranean, they were more noticeably oriental in character than the first phase cultures. However, there was a considerable degree of continuity from the first phase and, in addition, there was some absorption of local Mesolithic traits.

North European Plain route

This area is less well known than the other two and the main settlement was rather later in date.

The first well known culture in this area is the Tripolye culture found in southern Russia and south-east Europe. This culture, which was in existence by c. 4750 B.C. (C14 c. 4000 B.C.), is very oriental in appearance, with elaborate painted pottery and figurines, and seems to be related to the later painted ware groups of the Mediterranean and the Danubian II cultures in central Europe rather than to earlier groups.

In northern Europe itself the earliest Neolithic is the T.R.B. (or funnel-neck beaker) culture, sometimes known simply as the Northern Neolithic. This culture, which reached Denmark between c. 4100 and c. 3600 B.C. (C14 c. 3500–3000 B.C.) is the least oriental Early Neolithic culture in Europe (which is not surprising since it is both furthest away from the east and latest in date) and is characterised by pottery based on basketry traditions, timber long houses and the absence of oriental traits such as figurines. It appears to owe much to Mesolithic traditions. Specifically northern features include the mining of flint and the exploitation of Baltic amber. Elements of this culture appear to have crossed the North Sea and to have influenced the development of the British Neolithic (which was partly of Western Neolithic type). It is interesting that, although the L.B.K. culture of the Danubian group extended as far as Belgium and Holland, it did not cross the Channel to Britain. The reasons for this were probably environmental, the L.B.K. culture being adapted in the main to the loess soils of the central European river valleys, whereas the Western and Northern Neolithic cultures were adapted to conditions closer to those obtaining in lowland Britain.

So by 4000–3500 B.C. (C14 3500–3000 B.C.) Europe had been opened up by food-producers to the extremities of the area which could support primitive farming settlements. All the cultures discussed above were based on mixed farming, the main crops being emmer wheat and barley, the domesticated animals sheep, goat, cattle and swine. Beyond these areas, in the regions where the environment was too hostile to allow exploitation by primitive farming methods, peripheral groups of hunter–gatherers survived.

Subsequent developments

The period that followed the opening-up of Europe by farmers was very complicated and here I can only outline a few important trends.

(1) The continent of Europe was exploited on a much greater scale than previously. New resources, both living, in the form of new plant and animal foods, and mineral, such as flint, obsidian and hard rocks were exploited. Early farming methods involved wasteful destruction of vegetation and exhaustion of soil and under these pressures the face of Europe began to alter. For the first time in Europe man was materially altering his natural environment on a considerable scale.

(2) The expansion of population that followed the introduction of the farming economy, combined with the inefficient methods of primitive farming led to increasing density of settlement and to pressure on the land. The cultural consequence of this was increasing bellicosity, and the later Neolithic cultures of Europe tend to be characterised by fortified settlements and increasing numbers of weapons among the artefacts.

(3) Culturally the period is characterised by the fragmentation of the large culture-cycles of the earlier phases into numerous divergent groups, possibly reflecting adaptation to smaller regional environments.

(4) The Europeanisation of the cultures continued, as indicated by the development of specifically European cultural traits. The best example of this is the development of megalithic monuments in western Europe. At the height of this development, as exemplified by the decorated passage graves of Brittany, c. 4100–2500 B.C. (C14 3500–2000 B.C.), the cyclopean temples of Malta c. 3600–2500 B.C. (C14 3000–2000 B.C.) or the stone circles of the British Isles c. 3000–1750 B.C. (C14 2500–1500 B.C.), culminating in the magnificent monument of Stonehenge, these represent great achievements in terms of social co-operation and organisation, engineering

and, it seems now, in mathematical and astronomical observations (Thom 1967) (fig. 3). All these are distinctively European achievements, owing little or nothing to eastern inspiration (though this view is still not universally accepted), but all made possible by the liberating influence of the food-producing economy.

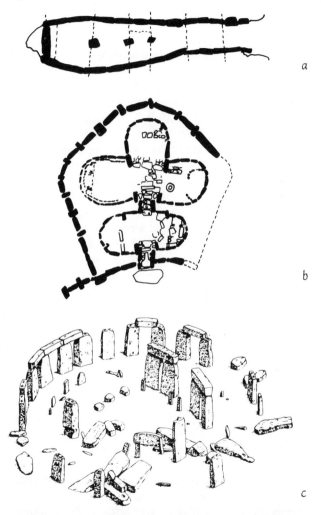

Fig. 3. Megalithic monuments: (a) plan of an Iberian passage grave (length of chamber c. 25 m.; (b) plan of Maltese temple (length along main axis is c. 100 m.; (c) isometric view of central area of Stonehenge (diameter c. 30 m.).

The development of megalithic monuments overlapped with the introduction and spread of metallurgy, which represents a new phase in the technological and economic development of Europe and which I shall therefore treat as a separate topic. First, however, I must return to the Near East to discuss the important developments which were taking place there, while Europe was being developed by early farmers.

The urban revolution

During the fourth millennium B.C., while Neolithic farmers were spreading the food-producing economy to the farthest corners of Europe, a second economic revolution was taking place in the Near and Middle East. Before 3000 B.C. this had transformed small settlements of farmers, self-sufficient in essentials, into large cities supported by secondary industries and foreign trade. As in the case of the food-producing revolution, this was the culmination of a long process and was 'revolutionary' only in its effects. Whereas farming was developed in the hill and plain zones of the Near East, the early urban communities arose in the river valleys where, with irrigation, very high crop yields could be attained and correspondingly high population densities supported. The three great ancient civilisations of the Old World arose on the alluvial soils of three very large river systems – the Tigris–Euphrates, the Nile and the Indus (fig. 4), but in smaller river valleys throughout the Middle East parallel developments towards urban life took place. The evolution of towns in Turkmenia has been studied in recent years (Masson 1968) and more recently still urban sites have been found also in Iran, at Shahr-i-Sokhta in Sistan and at Tepe Yaḥyā in Kerman province, where in 1970 very early tablets inscribed in the Proto-Elamite script were discovered (the Iranian sites are discussed in Lamberg-Karlovsky 1972). However, although urban communities developed initially wherever there were river valleys to be irrigated, it seems that only in the extremely large alluvial systems could the development be sustained and full civilisation emerge. Elsewhere, both in Turkmenia and south-eastern Iran, the urban communities were either abandoned subsequently or declined in status and civilisation was introduced from outside at a later stage.

Although irrigation agriculture was certainly the subsistence basis on which the early civilisations grew, the primacy of irrigation as a cause of the development is often challenged nowadays. Instead multicausal explanations are favoured and the urban revolution is seen as the result of the interaction of many factors. Some of the important factors are those emphasised by Childe (1936: Chapter VII): in the field of social organisation, the premium on social co-operation for the accomplishment of necessary tasks beyond the abilities of the individual or family, created by the difficult conditions of the alluvial valleys; in the sphere of technology, the invention of metallurgy and the wheel and the harnessing of animal and wind power; and in the field of trade, the necessity of organising efficient supplies of basic raw materials, such as stone, metal ores

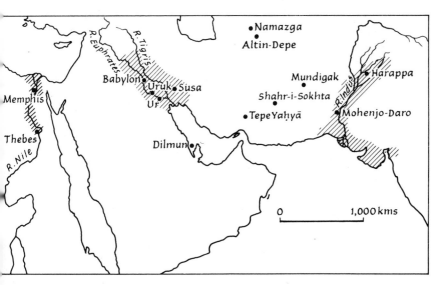

Fig. 4. The development of towns and the earliest civilisations.

and timber, which had to be brought from the highland zones adjacent to the river valleys. The greatly improved efficiency of primary production achieved by irrigation must still be regarded as a major factor in, though not the main cause of, the development of towns. The way in which these factors interacted can be illustrated by two examples. While the rich harvests allowed the accumulation of considerable surplus food, the premium on social co-operation led to the emergence of an organised leadership (on a religious basis in Mesopotamia, a military–political one in Egypt), which was able to concentrate this surplus; some of it was then made available for community projects such as maintenance of irrigation canals which were in their turn conducive to greater productivity in agriculture. Another example is provided by the technological developments,

39

which on the one hand contributed to greater efficiency in the exploitation of the environment and thus to the accumulation of a larger social surplus and, on the other hand, led to the growth of a class of specialist craftsmen and merchants, all of whom had to be supported out of this surplus. This kind of interaction has a multiplying effect, so that the process of urbanisation, once under way, gained in momentum as it progressed, leading to a rapid growth in population and an equally rapid development in social and economic organisation. The increasing complexity of community life, concentrated in the temples of Sumer and the royal courts of Egypt, gave rise to the invention of writing and developments in fields of knowledge such as mathematics, astronomy and medicine. So new classes of specialists – scribes and civil servants of various sorts – arose to join the craftsmen and merchants. Moreover the necessity of protecting the wealthy towns themselves and their external supplies of raw materials from envious and hostile neighbours led to the rise of professional armies, which also had to be supported out of communal funds.

So by 3000 B.C. we find in Egypt and Mesopotamia, and a little later in the Indus valley, true urban civilisations, literate and with a class society. As in the case of the development of farming, it is clear that there were connections between the three areas where urban civilisation arose, but that by and large the developments took place independently.

The influence of the urban revolution

By either of the definitions employed in this account the change from a fundamentally self-sufficient food-producing economy to one based on specialised manufacture and external trade counts as a revolutionary step in human progress. A considerable expansion of population is indicated by the size of both cities and cemeteries. And that there was a huge growth in the range of cultural activities cannot be doubted: there were developments of enormous importance in the fields of craft practice, theoretical knowledge, religion, architecture and art, among others, and the development of an entirely new form of communication – literature.

Civilisation, unlike the village farming economy which was the end product of the earlier revolution, was not a set of techniques and practices that could be extended without difficulty to large areas of the inhabited world. It was a complex organisation requiring at that stage a very rich natural environment to support it, a certain level of technological accomplishment and a certain degree of social development. However, even in areas where the full development could not take place, the influence of the urban civilisations made itself felt. Indeed in the areas immediately adjacent to the homeland, actual colonies, outposts of the civilisation itself, were established. Over a much larger area, however, the influence made itself felt through the medium of trade. Basic raw materials – metal ores, precious stones, timber etc. – were absent in the alluvial valleys and had to be brought from the highland zones, often over considerable distances. Wherever these materials occurred, there was an opportunity for the local inhabitants to make a profit, which came of course out of the accumulated surplus – the capital – of the civilised communities of the valleys. These peripheral communities in their turn could accumulate a surplus, support an increased population and develop economic specialisation. These new towns then served as secondary centres of capital, thus extending the process of influence outwards from the central area.

Childe believed that in this way we can explain not only the rise of urban communities in the Near and Middle East, but also in Europe, and he applied this explanation in detail to the Minoan–Mycenaean civilisation of the Aegean Bronze Age (Childe 1958: Chapter 7). Recently, however, Renfrew has argued cogently that the European civilisation was an independent and indigenous development, little influenced by contacts with the civilisations of the east (Renfrew 1972). However, even if there was little immediate influence on prehistoric Europe, the ancient civilisations and particularly that of Mesopotamia had in the long run a profound effect on European development. The impact was indirect and disparate, but through the media of classical Greece and Rome and the Jewish and Christian religions many elements of the knowledge, practice and beliefs of the Mesopotamian civilisation were incorporated, in transmuted form, into west European culture.

Economic and social development in Europe

The development of Europe differed considerably from that of the east. Primarily for environmental reasons there was never the same premium on co-operative effort as in the alluvial valleys where an individual or family had to join forces with its fellows or starve; under European conditions it was almost as easy for a family to farm on its own as in a larger community. The incentives for social development in this case were provided on the one hand by the pressure on the land after the initial Neolithic expansion, which forced people to live in larger communities and evolve social forms appropriate to these, and on the other by technological developments (the most important of which was metallurgy), which promoted economic specialisation. This led to some division of society on an economic basis, but because of the absence of the eastern premium on social co-operation and the much smaller dependence of society on imported goods for the functioning of its economy, there did not develop in Europe the rigid class society and divine leaders of the east. It was Childe's view (1958: 172–3) that in the long run this enabled European society to develop steadily and, from the classical period onwards, take over the cultural and political leadership of much of the known world, whereas eastern society having achieved the urban revolution in the first place eventually reached the point where progress was against the interests of the entrenched ruling classes and society remained more or less static.

As I have said, in Europe one of the main incentives to economic and social development was the development of technology, and one of the most important technological advances was the discovery of metallurgy. Until recently, it has always been thought that, like farming, metallurgy was developed outside Europe and was introduced from the Near East. However, very early C14 dates from eastern Europe suggest that it may have been developed there independently. It is true that smelted copper has been found in a seventh-millennium context in Anatolia, but the techniques did not become widespread in the Near and Middle East until the fifth or even the fourth millennium, by which stage there was a *more developed* industry in existence in the Balkans.

The practice of metallurgy was always dependent on the availability of raw materials, so in the first place its development in Europe was limited to areas where ores occurred, and outside these areas it was dependent at all times on imported materials. There were two main stages of development in Europe, which can be taken as approximately though not absolutely equivalent to:

(a) phase of copper metallurgy beginning in the fifth millennium;

(b) phase of bronze metallurgy (true tin bronze with 10 per cent tin) beginning in the late third millennium.

First phase of development of metallurgy

This took place in four main centres (fig. 5):

(1) *Eastern Europe.* There was already a developed copper industry in the Balkans in the fifth millennium B.C. (C14 fourth millennium). It was based on Transylvanian ores and comprised, as well as

42

ornaments, shaft-hole axes and axe-adzes. Indeed the calibrated C14 chronology makes these the earliest metal shaft-hole tools anywhere and it seems inescapable that this industry was developed locally (fig. 6a).

(2) *The Aegean*. This was a fairly well developed industry, based on ores occurring in eastern Crete and Cyprus, later on imported ores also. The repertoire included daggers (flat and with midribs), spearheads, axes and ornaments, all of copper, and also ornaments

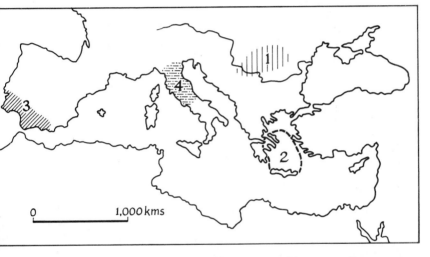

Fig. 5. Early centres of metallurgy in Europe: (1) eastern Europe; (2) the Aegean; (3) southern Iberia; (4) central and northern Italy.

of gold, silver and lead. This industry is often thought to be of Anatolian derivation, but it could be a local development. There are some late fourth-millennium metal finds, but the industry was not well established until the first half of the third millennium (C14 second half) (fig. 6b).

(3) *Southern Iberia*. Again based on local ores, this industry could also be a local development, although it is generally thought to be of Aegean inspiration. The suggestion that it was established by actual colonists from the Aegean is not acceptable: the Aegean parallels quoted for Iberian cultural traits do not belong to one chronological horizon or come from one area in the Aegean. The industry *could* be

43

derived from the Aegean, but could equally well be local: it includes daggers with midribs, as well as less distinctive forms such as flat daggers, flat axes and ornaments. As in the Aegean, metallurgy had begun in the fourth millennium B.C., but became well established only in the first half of the third millennium (C14 second half) (fig. 6c).

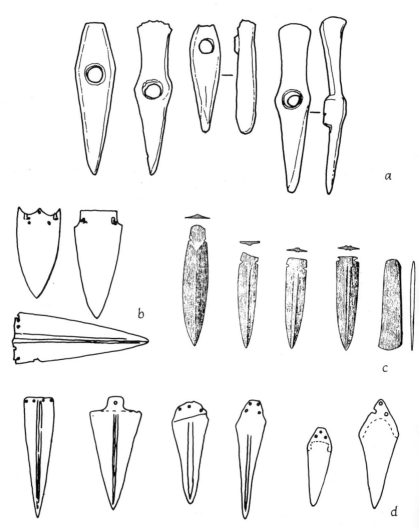

Fig. 6. Early metal types in Europe: (a) eastern Europe; (b) the Aegean; (c) southern Iberia; (d) central and northern Italy.

44

(4) *Central and northern Italy.* Also based on local ores, this industry can likewise be dated to the first half of the third millennium (C14 second half), with a few metal finds attributable to the previous millennium. It includes flat axes, flat daggers, triangular daggers with midribs with or without a tang, and halberds as well as generalised forms such as awls and simple ornaments. As for the Iberian group, an east Mediterranean origin has often been suggested for this industry, but a local origin is equally possible. In particular it has been suggested recently that the halberd form was developed in Italy (fig. 6d).

In any case these four early metal industries, whether developed locally or introduced from outside, were established within the context of existing Neolithic cultures (though this view is not universally held about the Aegean, Iberia or Italy). In all four areas they imply at least incipient economic specialisation, though initially this may only have meant a few itinerant smiths supported out of the accumulated social surplus of several different communities.

After the establishment of early metal-using communities, the development of the Aegean diverged from that of the rest of Europe. Whereas most of the continent underwent a period of cultural change, characterised by mobility of population, increasing bellicosity and increasing trade activities, but little economic or social advance, the Aegean communities were developing the urban civilisation we call after the Minoans and Mycenaeans.

Civilisation in the Aegean

Childe explained the development of urban life and civilisation in the Aegean, as everywhere else in Europe, in terms of the radiating influence of the urban civilisations of the east discussed above. Renfrew's new analysis, however, (Renfrew 1972) discounts influence from the east as a significant factor and argues that it evolved locally. Among the many factors contributing to this development Renfrew emphasises the crucial role of metallurgy and the development of a subsistence system which added the cultivated vine and olive to the cereal crops. The Minoan–Mycenaean civilisation is recognisable in Crete from c. 2000 B.C., but not on the mainland till c. 1600 B.C. at earliest. It was characterised by a bureaucratic system with the palace at the centre. The palaces were wealthy and supported large numbers of specialist craftsmen, merchants, civil servants etc.; the civilisation was literate and artistic and much of the craftsmanship was of a highly skilled quality. It flourished on the mainland till c. 1200 B.C., after which it disappeared almost

45

completely, possibly as a result of an invasion from the north, although environmental or internal social factors provide alternative explanations. Be that as it may, many of the towns were abandoned, urban life collapsed, writing ceased to be used and the fresh and naturalistic art styles gave way to repetitive and mechanical designs; the Mycenaean way of life survived only as half memory, half myth in the Homeric poems.

The Copper Age in Europe

During the period after the introduction of copper metallurgy, while urban life was slowly evolving in the Aegean, much of Europe was undergoing a sort of prehistoric 'migration period', characterised by movements of population of various sorts. This period was very complicated in detail, but in a simplified account one can see two main groups:

(1) *Eastern group*. Globular amphorae, Corded Ware, Battle-axe and Single-grave cultures. This group, which is found all over eastern and northern Europe may have an origin in the Kurgan culture of the south Russian steppes. Important traits shared by this group are single graves (often under barrows), wheeled vehicles, probably the domesticated horse, battle axes and copper metallurgy (fig. 7a). This group which had reached Holland by c. 3000 B.C. (C14 2500 B.C.), has been identified by some authorities with the Indo-Europeans (e.g. Piggott 1965: 85–97). The possession of the wheel and domesticated horses by this group are two features which make this group a plausible candidate for the hypothetical Proto-Indo-Europeans; however, it is debatable whether it is possible to equate archaeological with linguistic groups at all and it is certainly the case that some languages have spread without population movements on a significant scale.

(2) *Western group*. Beaker culture. This has a distribution in coastal Iberia, southern France, Sardinia, Sicily, northern Italy, eastern and central Europe, the Low Countries, Brittany and the British Isles, and there is really a remarkable similarity of material over this vast area. This group is characterised by typical beaker pottery, single graves under barrows (though this may not be an original trait), archers' equipment (flint arrowheads and stone wristguards) and copper metallurgy (fig. 7b). The origin of this group is disputed, many authorities favouring an Iberian homeland, but with some claims for an east European derivation. It must have been in

46

existence shortly after c. 3000 B.C. (C14 2500 B.C.). In the Low Countries it met and mixed with the Corded Ware tradition of the eastern group c. 2600–2500 B.C. (C14 2200–2100 B.C.) and most of the beakers found in the British Isles are the products of mixed Bell Beaker and Corded Ware traditions.

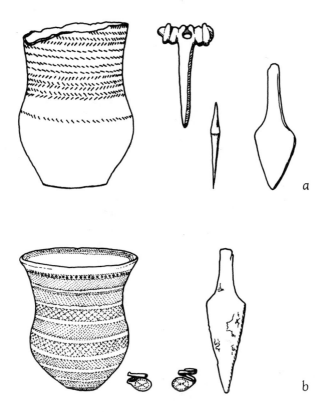

Fig. 7. Grave goods from tomb of (a) eastern group (East Germany) and (b) western group (Czechoslovakia).

These mobile groups, which seem to have often mixed freely with earlier groups (bell beakers, for instance, are frequently found in megalithic chamber tombs), were responsible for extending the knowledge of metallurgy from the areas where it was initially practised to the rest of Europe. In fact by c. 2000 B.C. (C14 1700 B.C.) the knowledge of metallurgy had been introduced almost to the extremities of inhabited Europe, to the British Isles and southern Scandinavia. However, metal was not very important to any

47

communities at this period, except possibly in the areas of origin discussed above. Other changes brought about by the mobile groups of this period include a shift of emphasis in subsistence economy towards pastoralism, increased bellicosity and increased trading activities; there may also have been changes in religious belief, with the earlier dominance of the mother goddess giving way to a sun cult, possibly reflecting, as do the warrior graves, a male-dominated society. There are, however, no indications of any division of society into classes on an economic basis.

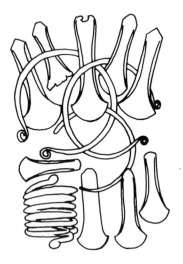

Fig. 8. Aunjetitz bronze types.

Second phase of development of metallurgy

Possibly as early as c. 2400 B.C. (C14 2000 B.C.), certainly by c. 2200 B.C. (C14 1850 B.C.), a more developed metal industry was established in southern central Europe, centred on Czechoslovakia. The industry and the culture associated with it are named after the site of Aunjetitz or Unetiče. The Aunjetitz industry, based on local ores, was technologically more advanced than the earlier Copper Age industries, being characterised by the use of true tin bronze, closed moulds etc. The typology of the artefacts of bronze also differed from those of the preceding period: the repertoire comprised low-flanged axes, triangular knife–dagger blades and solid-hilted daggers, halberds and ingot torques and a variety of bracelets, anklets and pins (fig. 8). A Near Eastern, more specifically a Syrian,

48

origin has been suggested for this industry (Childe 1957: 129), but the tree-ring calibration of C14 dates gives an earlier date for the European examples than for the supposed prototypes in the Near East; it seems probable that we must look for a local origin for the European Bronze Age, as for the Copper Age. Some features of the Aunjetitz culture certainly demonstrate continuity from the previous period, e.g. the use of single graves (sometimes under barrows) and some pottery forms.

Soon after the establishment of this industry in Czechoslovakia, it is found also in the neighbouring areas of southern Germany and Switzerland and there are contemporary groups in South-east Europe also. The next stage is characterised by the establishment of related industries in more distant areas where ores were available – northern Italy, Brittany, the British Isles etc. From this stage also imported metal goods were reaching areas without ores of their own – southern Italy, the Low Countries, Scandinavia etc. Subsequently, in what is roughly equivalent to the Middle Bronze Age in central Europe, c. 1700–1300 B.C. (C14 1500–1200 B.C.), local bronze industries were established even in these areas, based on imported materials.

This period – the Early and Middle Bronze Age – was a flourishing one for Europe, or at least for the better provided and more conveniently situated areas, characterised by technological progress and social prosperity. Childe saw this situation as a result of the radiating influence of the Mediterranean civilisations through the demands of the civilised societies for raw materials available in Europe. Of these the most in demand were the metal ores (copper and tin) of central and western Europe and the west Mediterranean and amber from the Baltic. However, these commodities were not traded in quantity before the Middle Bronze Age, and the Aegean trade can hardly have been a significant factor in the initial development of the European Bronze Age, though it may have contributed to its subsequent prosperity. More important, in all probability, was the trade within continental Europe itself which accompanied the practice of metallurgy and the social developments that followed it. As well as both increasing and distributing wealth, this trade spread technological know-how, and by the end of the Middle Bronze Age even the communities inhabiting areas without ores were practising metallurgical techniques as sophisticated as those in use in central Europe. The increasing wealth of this period meant that it was possible for societies to support more specialists than in earlier periods. It is clear that there were wealthy local chieftains, but in fact there is little evidence in the archaeological record for greater economic specialisation. Instead the evidence suggests that in some cases at least surplus wealth and energy were put into economically non-productive projects such as the erection of huge religious monuments like Stonehenge or the Carnac alignments. Doubtless too specialist priests were required to maintain these monuments and the cult and knowledge associated with them and these would have to be supported out of the social surplus. In strong contrast to the situation in the eastern civilisations, however, little if any of the social surplus was ploughed back into the community for *productive* purposes and therefore this period in Europe was characterised by little social advance.

The Late Bronze Age

The end of this phase in the development of Europe coincides with a phase of historically documented upheaval in the east Mediterranean and Near East, which saw the fall of the Hittite empire in Turkey and the fall of the Mycenaeans in the east Mediterranean, both in the half century c. 1200–1150 B.C. The relationship of events in Europe to those in the east Mediterranean is unclear and there is considerable dispute as to what was cause and what was effect. In central Europe this period saw the emergence of the Urnfield cultures of the Late Bronze Age, characterised by a more sophisticated industrial economy and more developed social forms than were found in the earlier Bronze Age. The adoption of the characteristic burial rite of these cultures – the dead were cremated and their ashes deposited in urns which were then laid in large cemeteries known as urnfields – and some of the metal types, such as swords, began as early as the thirteenth century B.C., but the main development of the cultures belongs to the five centuries following 1200 B.C. Early centres of Urnfield culture occurred in Hungary, Czechoslovakia and Austria and in the north Alpine area. The size and number of the cemeteries, the sophisticated techniques of bronze working and the organisation of the extraction of ores for the metal industry (true copper mines of this period are known, which must have employed a considerable number of people on a full-time basis) all suggest a greater population density and a more developed economy than in previous periods. It is probable that the basis on which this grew was a more efficient subsistence economy following the introduction on a wide scale of the plough (though this probably began to be used at an earlier stage in the Bronze Age) (fig. 9). This not only allowed more efficient exploitation of land already farmed, but made possible

50

the extension of agriculture to heavy soils such as clays, not previously cultivable. During this period bronze became much more common (perhaps partly because none was now being filtered off by the east Mediterranean market) and a wide variety of tools were now regularly made of metal for the first time – chisels, gouges, saws, sickles etc. – all of which must have increased the efficiency of many crafts and indeed of everyday activities of many sorts. Technological developments in the bronze industry include the beating of sheet bronze and core casting by the *cire perdue* method.

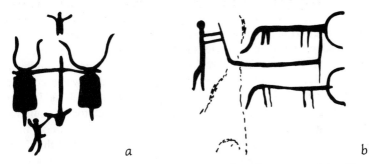

Fig. 9. Rock-engravings showing agricultural scenes: (a) Alpes Maritimes, France; (b) Valcamonica, Italy.

Urnfield expansion
The Urnfield period in Europe was characterised by another increase in population as a result of the increased efficiency of the economy. This led to expansion outside the area of origin and, as Europe was by now relatively densely populated, this was followed by displacement of populations previously existing in the regions into which the Urnfield peoples now expanded, so that population movements of one kind or another affected a large part of Europe. In addition to these movements, Urnfield ideas and practices also spread through the medium of trade. So, through a combination of migration and diffusion the Urnfield economy or a version of it was spread over most of Europe. By the Late Bronze Age (varying in date from c. 1200 B.C. in central Europe to c. 800 B.C. in outlying areas) we find in most regions a consolidated system of settled farming, based on plough agriculture combined with stock-breeding and an economic organisation with, in all probability, specialist smiths in each community replacing the travelling tinkers of earlier periods. It was at this time that the first of the European hillforts were constructed; these were hilltop settlements surrounded by earth,

51

or earth and timber, ramparts and they became the most characteristic form of settlement during the Iron Age.

The introduction of iron

Iron technology was initially a jealously guarded secret of the Hittite
kings and it was not until the fall of the Hittite empire in Turkey
early in the twelfth century B.C. that iron-working began to spread.
It spread initially to the coasts and islands of the east Mediterranean,
had reached Greece by the eleventh or tenth centuries, Italy by the
ninth, eastern and central Europe by the eighth or seventh centuries
and western Europe a century or so later. The production of iron is
more difficult than that of bronze, but once the technology had been
mastered, because of the widespread availability of iron ores (in
contrast to the restricted distribution of those of copper and still
more so of tin), it became a very cheap metal and thus was used from
the beginning, unlike bronze, not only for weapons such as daggers
and swords and for basic tools such as axes, but for agricultural
implements such as sickles, ploughs and hoes. This must have
greatly increased the efficiency of agricultural practice and thus contributed to the support of larger communities practising greater
economic specialisation. The spread of iron technology seems to
have taken place largely by diffusion through the medium of trade,
though in central Europe it may have been partly introduced by
small groups of immigrants from the east and in some parts of the
central and west Mediterranean it was introduced by Phoenician or
Greek colonists.

The spread of civilisation

After the collapse of the Mycenaean and Hittite powers shortly after
c. 1200 B.C. the Phoenician civilisation of the Levantine coast
emerged as a maritime power in the Mediterranean. Perhaps already
in the second millennium B.C. and certainly by the ninth century the
Phoenicians were establishing colonies in the central and west
Mediterranean, the most famous of which was Carthage, which
became a long-standing enemy of Rome. The most enduring
contribution of the Phoenicians was their alphabetic script, which
indeed forms the basis of both the Latin and the Arabic scripts in use
today. By the eighth century Greece had emerged from the 'Dark
Ages' that followed the fall of Mycenae and a fully developed urban
civilisation was establishing colonies on the Black Sea and, in
competition with the Phoenicians, in the central and west
Mediterranean. Meanwhile the rich Urnfield-based Villanovan

culture of central Italy was developing towards a true urban civilisation its own, with the help of oriental influences derived from extensive trading contacts with both Greeks and Phoenicians. By the end of the eighth century the historical Etruscans are recognisable in the archaeological record. In the succeeding two centuries they expanded to gain control over much of north and central Italy and became a significant power in the central Mediterranean – as both Phoenician and Greek traders and colonists discovered. Both classical Greek and Etruscan civilisations were characterised by a city-dwelling, highly organised class society, literate and artistic, organised politically in self-governing cities. In the long run this political system led to the decline of the civilisation, and in the case of the Etruscans its actual eclipse. However, much of its economic and social structure and many cultural traits were taken over by its destroyer, Rome, which, in spite of its deliberate adoption of the heritage of Greece, was in many senses the heir of the Etruscans.

The Mediterranean civilisations of Greece and Etruria had a profound influence on the Iron Age cultures of Europe, of which the best known is that named after the Austrian site of Hallstatt (dated c. 700–500/450 B.C.), which developed directly out of the local Urnfield culture. Once again, as in the period before 1200 B.C., the demand of the Mediterranean civilisations for metal ores, amber and other products allowed European communities to supplement the products of their own economy by trade with the Mediterranean world. Imported goods, local imitations and their derivatives are common on Hallstatt settlement sites, many of which were hillforts, and especially in their cemeteries. Greek and Etruscan fashions in the trappings of warfare, the practice of wine drinking and personal ornament were adopted by the courts of the wealthy Hallstatt chieftains and developed to produce distinctively European forms; on one German hillfort a Mediterranean style of defence built with mudbrick was adopted, only to be abandoned when it proved unsuitable for central European conditions (fig. 10). In the earlier phase most of the trade and accompanying influences passed from the head of the Adriatic up the old amber routes into central Europe, but after the foundation of the Greek colony of Massilia (Marseilles) c. 600 B.C., and especially from c. 550 B.C., the emphasis shifted westwards, and most of the Mediterranean goods and influences spread up the Rhône and Saône and across to the Rhine and the Danube. On the basis of the efficient Urnfield-inherited subsistence economy and the Mediterranean trade, the successors of the Hallstatt chieftains in western Europe, named after the Swiss site of

La Tène, developed a rich culture which borrowed much from the civilisations of the Mediterranean. By the third and second centuries B.C. the hillforts had grown into large *oppida* (of which the most famous example is Manching) which were true towns with a high population density and a class society with wealthy chieftains and their courts, many specialist craftsmen – workers in metal, pottery, glass etc. – the basic peasant population and, it seems, a stratum of

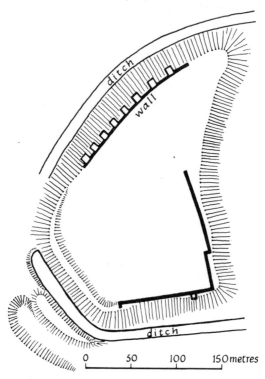

Fig. 10. Plan of the Heuneberg hillfort, Germany, with bastioned wall of stone and mudbrick.

slaves, acquired through inter-tribal warfare. The adoption in the second century B.C. of a coin currency on a tribal basis marks a significant development in both economic and political organisation. In the less prosperous peripheral areas of Europe we find varying degrees of development towards an urban economy of this kind. Indeed large parts of Europe had to wait for the arrival of the imperial forces of Rome for the forcible establishment of a viable urban economy. This was finally achieved everywhere within the limits of the Roman Empire in Europe by about the end of the first century A.D.

As chapter 3 will show, the advent of the Roman Empire marked an important stage in the development of Europe. The establishment of urban civilisation brought with it material prosperity (based on more efficient farming techniques and the new secondary industries), political security (upheld by the imperial armies) and new technological skills. This led to great developments in many fields, such as civil engineering, architecture, many crafts and the arts – especially literature; in addition more complex forms of social organisation were introduced and evolved. In cultural terms this period is often regarded as the beginning of the modern era. In spite of the eclipse of many facets of civilised life during the Dark Ages in western Europe, the survival of the Empire in the east and the revival of classical institutions and skills in the west from the Carolingian Renaissance onwards meant that our own culture owes a considerable debt to the classical civilisation of Greece and Rome.

3

The Roman Period

Martin Henig

INTRODUCTION

It is hard to exaggerate the importance of the Roman Empire for the development of Europe. During the four hundred years of its existence traditional ways of life were swept away and replaced by more complex forms of social organisation. Our very words 'city', 'civilisation', 'urban' and 'community' have Latin roots and thus demonstrate the close association between Roman culture and the town. Only in such an environment was it possible for the majority of men to forget their immediate struggle with nature and develop the arts of peace, above all those associated with literacy. The great difference between the beginning of the Bronze Age and the beginning of the Roman period is that the latter did not usher in the use of new materials to any significant extent even if some, such as stone and pottery, were used with far greater competence than before. In fact, the Iron Age continued, although it seems pedantic to use the term for either the Roman period or for any of the succeeding phases of western history.

Even where cities already existed in the Near East, Greece and Eturia, the Pax Romana made a great difference. Never before had it been possible to travel from Scotland to the Persian Gulf and from the Danube to the wastes of the Sahara along well-built roads without crossing anything more than the occasional provincial frontier. The Romans were justly proud of this and as early as the late first century B.C., Virgil defined the Roman mission as 'to bear dominion over the nations and to impose the law of peace, to spare the conquered and put down the proud'.

ROME AND 'ANTIQUITY'

It is a common mistake to approach Roman civilisation with the aim of contrasting it unfavourably with the world of classical Greece. In truth Greece and Rome form a cultural continuum: from the eighth

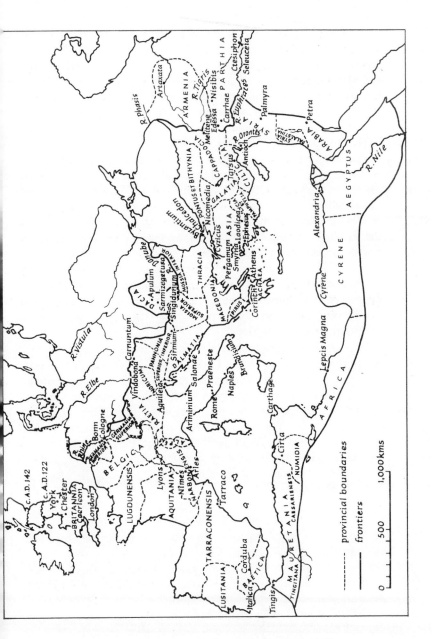

Fig. 1. The Roman Empire in the second century A.D.

to the fourth centuries the culture of antiquity was born in the South Balkans and Asia Minor (and was also carried to South Italy); in the fourth century Alexander III of Macedon, after conquering Egypt and the Levant, began the 'Hellenisation' of the former Persian Empire. Finally, through the agency of Rome, Greek culture was carried to every land that borders on the Mediterranean and even to some (e.g. Britain) beyond it.

The Roman Empire, far from eclipsing Greece, saw the triumph of Hellenism. Greek was as much a major language of the Empire as Latin; Greek art, Greek religion and Greek ethics were everywhere very much in evidence. One of the greatest works of philosophy produced in antiquity is the volume of meditations written *in Greek* by the Roman Emperor Marcus Aurelius. Some of the loveliest statues ever produced by Greek artists celebrate the beauty of Hadrian's young friend Antinous, drowned in the Nile (A.D. 130) and subsequently the object of fervent religious veneration. Naturally it is absurd to maintain that Hadrian's appreciation of human perfection and Marcus Aurelius' conception of divine law detracted from their 'Roman' qualities as administrators and soldiers.

When the future governor of Britain, Cn. Julius Agricola, was sent to university, he went to the Greek city of Marseilles. The fourth-century Emperor Julian studied at Athens and, as is evident from his writings, was more of a Greek than a Latin speaker – he was dragged to the imperial throne murmuring some lines of Homer about 'purple death' – but he achieved enormous popularity in Gaul where he expelled the Teutonic invaders and thus gave the western Roman Empire another century of rather shaky existence. Julian's biographer Ammianus Marcellinus, 'a Greek' as he describes himself, was the author of the best Latin History since Tacitus. Antique civilisation did not perish with the fall of the Roman Empire in the west, for Constantinople (the city of Constantine, also known as Byzantium) continued to be the capital of emperors who traced their pedigrees to Augustus. Even if they no longer spoke Latin, their subjects were still *Romanoi*. Here Homer and Euripides were quoted as a matter of course, and something of the cultural legacy of ancient Greece was preserved for posterity.

Greece, Rome (and perhaps even the early years of Byzantium) are still commonly given the same generic name, antiquity. It is true that the periods dealt with in the first two sections of this book have, in strict logic, as good a right to the term, but the cultures of prehistory only became subjects deemed worthy of scholarly study in the comparatively recent past, while the memory of Greece and Rome was never lost (although it was sometimes dim during the centuries between the collapse of the western Empire and the Renaissance). Even two hundred years ago, the ideals of the civilised man were those of the ancient world.

A culture in which Greek and Latin authors were read in the original and freely translated, which adapted its architecture to accord with the canons of Vitruvius, and even educated its youth in a manner which would have been familiar to Cicero, Quintilian or Ausonius, has a right to consider itself as the heir to the ancient world, although far removed from it in time.

Antique ideals

Antiquity can be distinguished from the barbarian world (the word barbarian like the word civilisation is derived from an ancient term, in this case a Greek one: non-Greeks spoke unintelligibly, *bar-bar*), not only through its complex organisation and literacy, which were in any case features of the civilisations of the Near East, but also for its liberal and humanistic values. As early as the Homeric poems which achieved their final form in the eighth century B.C., the gods are described as though they were built in the image of man. They are ever young and ever beautiful, unlike the deities of many ancient peoples who were conceived in hideous or animal forms or, like the god of the Hebrews, were not depicted at all. Man only differed from the eternally happy gods in one important and tragic respect: he was mortal:

> Suns that set, may rise again,
> But if once we lose this light
> 'Tis with us perpetual night
> (Catullus, trans. Ben Jonson)

In the eighth century the Olympic Games became a prominent institution. These ancient games were genuine religious occasions in which men contended for glory alone. The prize, a chaplet of wild olive, was only won through the assistance of the god. Contenders in the races ran naked; this had something to do with ritual purity, but the essential idea, that man should not be ashamed of his body, ran counter to the taboos of Near Eastern society and was consequently a revolutionary innovation. Greek gods and heroes are usually shown nude in art – there are good early examples in the seventh century 'youths' (or *kouroi*). Unlike the medieval church obsessed with man's sinfulness and fall from grace, Greek religion was concerned with human perfection insofar as mortals subject to fate

59

could ever be perfect. The Romans with their (originally) more primitive ideas and love of ritual for its own sake were, nevertheless, forced to incorporate the Greek conception of religion into their own. The simple, rural godlings of the Italian countryside became the fair, shining deities of Mt Olympus.

It followed that because man, like the gods, had personality and reason every individual had the right, and indeed the duty, to participate in the public life of his community. Although women, slaves and foreigners were excluded from it as a matter of course, every Greek state had some sort of franchise. However there were obviously great differences between democracies (such as Athens) and oligarchies (for example Sparta and Corinth).

In the former, effective power was exercised through the assembly of all free adult citizens; in the latter only the wealthier and more aristocratic residents had much say in forming policy, and the town council (*Boule*) was much more important than the assembly.

Until Alexander the Great, king of the partially Hellenised state of Macedonia, conquered almost the entire known east and brought it into the Greek world, there was a strong vein of racial exclusiveness amongst the Greeks. This may have been in part because they were conscious of the power of their enemies, especially Persia, which had so nearly subjugated Greece in the early fifth century B.C. There is much truth in Sir Mortimer Wheeler's opinion that Alexander was virtually the first Roman Emperor. Certainly, from his time onwards the imperial burden which Rome would assume – the mission to civilise the entire world – was there for all to see.

The history of the Roman Republic is full of interest to the student of human institutions, although outside Italy its influence was slight until the third century B.C. when the Carthaginians were defeated and Roman control was established over Sicily, Sardinia and a part of Spain. In the following century territories in Africa, the east, and southern France were added so that Rome suddenly found herself a world power. Unlike Alexander's Empire, the product of one man's genius, the Roman Empire was founded by a city ruled, officially at any rate, by a senate of notables and by a popular assembly; in practice, power resided in the hands of the most influential families in the former body and with the best demagogues in the latter. Although this system worked well enough for a time it could not last for ever. Paradoxically, at the very moment that Rome was about to spread the Greek system of self-governing cities further than it had ever been spread before by founding *coloniae* and *municipia* in distant lands, her own constitution collapsed, only to be restored in a form remarkably like that of Alexander's Empire and of the kingdoms which succeeded it in Macedonia, Syria and Egypt.

The Civil War

The epic story of the end of the Republic, as momentous to future ages as the Trojan War or the Persian Wars, is known throughout the English speaking world through Shakespeare's plays *Julius Caesar* and *Antony and Cleopatra* (which are, incidentally, not only amongst the greatest dramas in the English language, but exciting historical reconstructions, including insights into character and psychology that actually illuminate the ancient historians). Julius Caesar conquered central and northern France and then defeated his rival, Pompey the Great, in civil war. Excited by ambition, though not dominated by it, he played with the idea of monarchy. This was enough to alarm his rivals and Caesar was assassinated on the Ides of March 44 B.C. In the Civil War that followed, it was Caesar's heirs who triumphed.

At first Octavian, Lepidus and Antony attempted to rule the Roman world as a triumvirate, but Lepidus lacked the necessary dynamism and personality and fell from power in 36 B.C., while Mark Antony thought 'the world well lost' for Cleopatra. There is something fitting in the fact that the last great Roman general before the Augustan principate should perish (after the Battle of Actium 31 B.C.) fighting as much for the honour of Cleopatra, the last of the Hellenistic monarchs, as for himself. In 27 B.C. Octavian regularised his position vis-à-vis the Senate (his nominal partner) and took the title Augustus.

PROVINCIAL GOVERNMENT UNDER THE EMPIRE

The government of the Empire was usually fair and reliable in the provinces where the fact that the central administration was unchanged from year to year had definite advantages: governors were directly accountable to the emperor and had to bear his praise or censure. There is a famous anecdote about the Emperor Tiberius who accused a governor of overtaxing provincials: 'I asked you to shear my sheep, not to flay them.' It must be remembered, with regard to the cities, that the only outside authority would be exercised through the governor (*Legatus Augusti pro praetore*) and the financial officer (*procurator*); in most cases, apart from taxation, they were substantially free.

Tacitus records a famous speech by the general Cerialis,

61

addressing two Gallic tribes which revolted in A.D. 70, which lists some of the advantages of the Pax Romana.

> 'Never was Gaul without wars and kingships until you came under the rule of Rome; and we Romans though provoked so often, have exercised no victors' rights save that of maintaining peace. For there can be no peace without armies; no armies without pay, and no pay without tribute: all else is held in common between us. You yourselves are often in command of our Legions; you yourselves may be Governors of these and other Provinces; nothing is closed or barred against you. The benefits enjoyed under good Emperors you enjoy equally with others, though you live so far away; the cruelties of bad Emperors fall upon those who are on the spot...Be lovers therefore of Peace; love and revere the city which belongs, by equal right, to conquerors and to conquered.'
>
> (Tacitus: *Histories* Book IV. 74, trans. G. G. Ramsay)

Tacitus, here less cynical than usual, shows that the Roman Empire actually brought freedom. This must have included political freedom, for there was strong competition to become a member of the local council (*ordo*) and eventually to be elected one of the two chief magistrates (*duoviri*) who held office for a year. There was of course freedom to trade, freedom from war, and above all freedom to amuse oneself – colonnaded streets, baths and elegant banquets are all mentioned by Tacitus in his *Agricola* as being features of life in a British town during the Flavian period (c. A.D. 79).

A fine example of such a colonnade is known from Lincoln which has also yielded the remains of an aqueduct that supplied water to the baths and public fountains of the *colonia*. Important first-century bath buildings have been excavated at Silchester (Neronian) and Wroxeter (Late Flavian) (fig. 2). Banquets are less easy to illustrate archaeologically. Normally they will have taken place in the dining rooms (*triclinia*) of private houses; these would have been decorated with mosaics and wall-paintings such as those unearthed at Verulamium and Leicester, dating from the second century A.D.

'The far flung battle line'

Kipling's famous *Recessional* would have appealed to the better Roman administrators. Like the British, the Romans saw their tasks in religious terms and, while proclaiming the eternity of their dominion, they knew that it would one day end. For Marcus Aurelius, Asia and Europe were merely corners of the Universe.

'Everything which you see will be changed by Nature that controls the Universe . . . so that the world may renew its youth.' For a Stoic such as Marcus, the exercise of responsibility with righteousness carried its own reward. Such a philosophy may seem bleak, but it is characteristically Roman.

During the reign of Augustus the frontiers of the Empire were fixed, to all intents and purposes: the defeat of P. Quinctilius Varus in A.D. 9 ensured that the Rhine and not the Elbe was to be the limit of Roman control in Germany. Britain was conquered under Claudius and his successors (A.D. 43 onwards) and Dacia (Romania) was subdued by Trajan in the early second century.

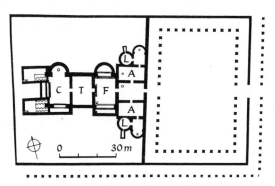

Fig. 2. Plan of the public baths at Wroxeter, Shropshire; first Century A.D. A = undressing room; C = hot room; F = cool room; L = 'Spartan' room of intense dry heat; T = room of moderate heat.

The organisation and settlement of this vast area happened more slowly. For the most part the army was stationed on the frontiers, with native auxiliary troops in forward positions and the legions in their fortresses to the rear. The army served a triple function: it defended the Roman world against the barbarians, it controlled unruly areas and brought civilisation to them and finally, by taking provincials into the auxiliary regiments, it trained men for the responsibilities of Roman citizenship. In the army the recruit could learn many a skilled trade, from medicine to pottery manufacture, from clerical work to blacksmithing.

Even in areas behind the frontiers, the Roman archaeologist cannot forget the Imperial Army: it has been suggested that Romano-British *fora* (fig. 3) were adapted from military *principia* while the earliest shops at Verulamium (see fig. 4) are very like the store

63

buildings found in first-century forts. Furthermore at some stage or other of its history every province had seen the presence of a Roman army of invasion and in Britain good examples of early (i.e. first-century) forts have been excavated at Hod Hill and Waddon Hill in Dorset, Richborough in Kent, and Great Casterton in Rutland.

The towns

Within the frontiers the provinces were largely agricultural. Industry was light and even the samian-ware potteries of central Gaul and the silver mines in Spain were comparatively small enterprises by modern standards. The countryside was always underprivileged compared with the towns. Although the Roman poets are rightly considered as having a good eye for scenery, there is something

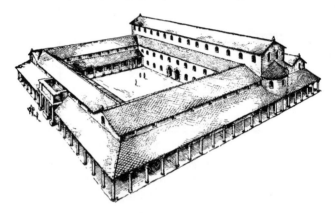

Fig. 3. Reconstruction of the forum and basilica at Silchester, Hampshire, c. A.D. 100.

artificial (or at least dilettante) in many of their descriptions. Nor is this surprising, for only a city dweller would romanticise the countryside as Virgil and Horace, for example, certainly do. The villas of the rich carried the comforts of the city out into the wilds, just as the town houses of Pompeii include rooms frescoed with landscape scenes and gardens that imitate an ordered countryside on a small scale; but both villas and gardens point to the distance between town and country, not to their closeness.

The foundation of towns and the construction of roads between them may be counted amongst the most permanent and significant contributions made by Rome to the future development of Europe. Even in Britain, where cities were often remodelled in the early middle ages (M. Biddle and D. Hill, 'Late Saxon Planned Towns', *Antiquaries Journal* LI (1971), 70–85), this is true. It is rare to find the sites of Roman cities so completely abandoned as Silchester or Wroxeter, and although the *municipium* of Verulamium has given way to the city of St Albans (centred on the probable site of the saint's martyrdom in the early third century A.D.) and Cirencester, the second largest city of Roman Britain, has now shrunk to a position of comparative unimportance, we have to weigh this against the success of such thriving centres as Winchester, Exeter, Canterbury, York and (above all) London. Indeed a limiting factor in our knowledge and understanding of the early history of urbanisation in Britain is the very success of the Roman foundations. Roman London achieved a size of 330 acres, which was hardly to be exceeded in the Middle Ages, and the same rapid growth rate is true for other towns as well. The fourth century imperial capital of Trier, over twice as large as London, has remained a notable city until this day, but after the fall of the western Empire, never regained its old importance for all the prestige implied by its medieval title, *sancta civitas Treverorum.*

The problem of institutional continuity is a difficult one. In the towns of Gaul, Germany, Spain and Italy there are churches dating from the late Roman period and the succeeding dark ages. Furthermore there is frequently literary evidence to show that such places as Poitiers, Tours, Cologne, Merida and Barcelona have a continuous existence from the time of their foundation onwards. In Britain, although scholars no longer believe that the towns were suddenly deserted in the early fifth century, there is little evidence for a vigorous civic life after the visit of St Germanus (A.D. 429). The Anglo-Saxon poem, *The Ruin,* suggests that at some time, perhaps in the sixth century, it was possible to look upon Bath as the work of a race of giants. However, magnificent sites and great buildings (still standing in Saxon times, as attested by Bede in his life of St Cuthbert with regard to Carlisle and as evidenced by archaeological excavation in the case of York) were an abiding legacy to the future.

Many professions were practised in the Roman city. The lawyers stood at the top of the social ladder, and many members of the aristocracy in both republican and imperial times were barristers. Lecturers (in such university towns as Autun, Marseilles, Athens and Alexandria) were also respected, although at more elementary levels school-teaching does not seem to have been held in much regard. Medicine and architecture were acceptable skills, but sculpture ranked with the artisan trades. However, despite its low status, this craft has left a legacy of fine reliefs showing scenes from daily life. It is evident that studios were locally based (as were those of mosaic workers) and much useful work is possible on the various schools of craftsmen practising in different parts of the Empire.

Most of the urban population was engaged in trade, and with the exception of a few rich merchants (importing spices or gems from the Far East, wine from Spain or luxury goods from Italy) these were poor men, content with a modest profit.

Their narrow dwellings, partly open to the street, served both for accommodation and for business. Indeed the artisan quarters of a Roman town would look very similar to such a district in a medieval city, or even a Mediterranean one at this day (fig. 4).

Fig. 4. Reconstruction of mid first-century shops at Verulamium (St Albans), Hertfordshire.

Evidence for their life and work comes from grave reliefs mentioned above, such as those found at Trier, Arlon and Bordeaux and from the archaeological examination of workshops. We may note a goldsmith's workshop in London; a silver refinery at Silchester; a glass factory at Caister St Edmund and pottery kilns (some making samian) at Colchester.

This lower middle class was the backbone of the community; it had to be pampered through the provision of public fountains, baths, theatre shows, horse-races and above all gladiatorial displays. Because of the wise provision of 'bread and circuses', there was, as Tacitus realised not without a certain scorn, remarkably little social unrest – until, that is, the inflation and political troubles of the third century disorganised and disrupted urban life. The Empire's strength

66

was always in its cities. Where they held their own in the east, culture on a high level could continue; in the west most cities never truly recovered and the Empire was doomed.

ARCHAEOLOGY AND THE EMPIRE

So far this account, although intended primarily for students of archaeology has hardly been concerned with excavation. This is because, for the Roman period, it is not possible to take a strictly scientific approach. History often dictates what the archaeologist will find, and the dating of structures must take account of historical events. Thus, to take one example, Tacitus says that Agricola spent the winter of A.D. 79 building *fora*. At Verulamium in Hertfordshire an inscription actually dates the *forum* to this year. In London the latest Gaulish red-gloss pottery found in the pre-forum levels belongs

Fig. 5. Dedication to Serapis from York; second century A.D.

to the early Flavian period. It is thus probable that it, too, dates to the year A.D. 79. Such an assumption demands a little knowledge of classical sources and of ancient history.

In York an inscription set up by Claudius Hieronymianus, legate of the sixth Legion, records that he erected a temple to the Egyptian god Serapis (fig. 5). We know Hieronymianus from a work by Tertullian which says that when he was a governor in Cappadocia in Asia Minor, he persecuted the Christians. Evidently he realised that Christianity was a rival to his own particular faith. Again, history and archaeology illuminate one another.

In a prehistoric excavation there is seldom any chance of being able to know for certain what a particular structure was used for, but we know that a Roman temple excavated in London was dedicated to Mithras, a Persian god, and that Hadrian built the Wall named after him.

However, pure excavation and the study of extant monuments obviously has its value. Temples in Britain are often dissimilar from temples in Turkey or Italy; the native religion in Judaea is evidently very different from the native cults of Gaul. It is as well to sample the various remains found in the provinces and to hint at their diversity. There is no space to do more, and there are, in any case, numerous general surveys dealing with classical archaeology, some of which are listed in the bibliography.

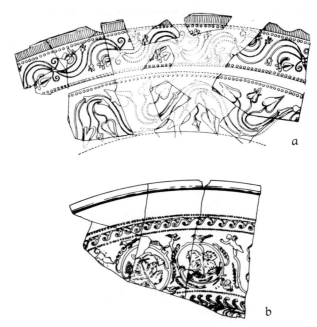

Fig. 6. Figured samian from Fishbourne, Sussex. (a) Form 29, c. A.D. 40–55. (b) Form 37, c. A.D. 100–200.

Artefacts

The first thing to strike anyone accustomed to excavating on prehistoric sites is the abundance of remains (pottery, metal trinkets, coins etc.) which even an ordinary Roman site tends to yield. More people owned more possessions for the simple reason that mass production had come to replace the efforts of the solitary craftsman; the corollary of this fact is that where comparable objects were made in the late prehistoric period and in the Roman age, a sharp drop in quality can be observed. We have only to compare the bold invention of the Celtic shields from Battersea and Wandsworth with the conventional ornament found on so many pieces of Romano-

British metalwork. It is interesting to note that one of the fine British mirrors with engraved back, manufactured early in the first century A.D., was found in Nijmegen, Holland where it was probably lost by a soldier of Legio IX Hispana in the second century: the object had clearly been cherished as an heirloom.

Much of the pottery found on first- and second-century sites in Britain is of a red fabric with glossy finish. Sometimes the vessels are plain but others are decorated with figured and animal designs in

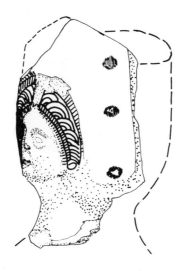

Fig. 7. Face mask from a flagon; from Toot Baldon, Oxfordshire. Third or fourth century A.D. Height c. 16 cms.

relief (fig. 6). We call all these vessels samian (because the elder Pliny describes a type of red pottery made in Samos) but it is now known that they were made in Gaul at such sites as La Gaufesenque in the south and Lezoux in the centre.

Other types of pottery were actually made in Britain, and there are important kiln sites near Stanmore, Middlesex; Rossington Bridge near Doncaster, Yorkshire; in the New Forest, Hampshire and in the Nene Valley, Northamptonshire. Some 'coarse' wares are decorated. A group of flagons ornamented with female heads are especially worthy of mention. Recent work carried out on these vessels by Mr Julian Munby suggests that some of the best were made in Oxfordshire kilns whence they were exported widely, to London and to Lydney, Gloucestershire for example (fig. 7). Pottery is often closely datable because specimens of the same type have been found in association with coins in mint condition.

Coins were struck at various times and in many places throughout the Empire (though particularly at Rome) (fig. 8). However, they circulated widely, and few monetary systems can ever have been so successful as that which flourished in the first and second centuries A.D. The gold piece (*aureus*) is seldom found on excavations, but the silver *denarius* (worth one-twentieth of an *aureus*) and the base-metal *sestertii* and *asses* into which this coin was divided are often found. One side of a Roman imperial coin always shows the Emperor's

TRUSSEL

COIN
LOWER DIE
PILE
ANVIL

Fig. 8. Coin die (Hadrianic, c. A.D. 134–8) used for striking denarii. Found at Verulamium, Hertfordshire. (The type shows Hadrian being received by Roma, within the legend Adventus Aug.*)*

head or that of another member of his family with his or her name and titles forming a surrounding legend. The other face is devoted to the portrayal of a god, attribute, emblem or item of state propaganda, so that as well as yielding evidence for the date of archaeological sites, coins provide a convenient official government 'history' of Rome.

Agricultural implements (and other tools) are not infrequently encountered on excavations where the soil conditions allow iron to be preserved satisfactorily. These help us to understand how many a Roman artisan spent his day, and K. D. White has done a valuable service in matching up surviving implements with ancient texts that describe them. (K. D. White, *Agricultural Implements of the Roman World* (Cambridge 1967).) As far as Britain is concerned one might single out the remarkable hoard of ironwork from Great

70

Chesterford, Essex, now in the Cambridge University Museum of Archaeology and Ethnology.

Personal ornaments, brooches and finger-rings are also worthy of study for anyone interested in the history of taste. Early Roman ornament tends to be rather simple, but in the third century (and even more in the fourth) jewellery becomes heavier and more elaborate. Compare the bracelets, necklaces and rings from Pompeii with their equivalents from Ténès (Algeria), Tarsus or Palmyra. Engraved gems used as signets have a very special significance, for if coin-types are the public seals of the state, these sum up the private individual's interests and aspirations. A soldier might select Mars, god of War, or a legendary hero such as Achilles or Theseus, while a Christian could well employ the Good Shepherd as his device (cf. my paper in *Britannia* I (1970), 249–65) (fig. 9).

To mention every type of object which can be found on Roman sites would take up too much space, but religious dedications must not be left out. A good example is the bronze statuette of Mars from the Foss Dyke, Lincolnshire, which is set on a base inscribed. 'To the god Mars and to the Numina [i.e. deities] of the Emperors, the Colasuni [? brothers] Bruccius and Caratius, presented this at their own expense at a cost of a hundred sestertii; Celatus the coppersmith fashioned it and gave a pound of bronze made at the cost of three denarii' (*R.I.B.* 274). Alongside such an explicit inscription as this we must set the many stone sculptures and small bronzes from temple sites whose mode of dedication is unknown. Who gave the head of Serapis to the London Mithraeum or the fine relief of the Celtic Genii Cucullati to a small shrine at Housesteads? Under what circumstances were the figurines of hounds given to the god Nodens at Lydney; and who could afford the excellent bronze figure of Mercury found at a temple site at Gosbecks' Farm near Colchester?

A BRIEF ARCHITECTURAL TOUR
OF THE PROVINCES

Britain

From the archaeologist's point of view Britain is amongst the most productive of provinces because of the number of excavations carried out every year and the increasingly high standards of the techniques employed. There are few monuments which are really well preserved but some sections of Hadrian's Wall, the Saxon Shore Forts of Richborough, Pevensey, and Portchester, the late fortlet of Caer Gybi on the Isle of Anglesey, the military amphitheatres at

71

Caerleon and Chester, the Lighthouse at Dover, the Great Bath at Bath, the Palace of Fishbourne and the villas of Chedworth, Bignor and Lullingstone are all worth a visit. A large proportion of the surviving monuments of Britain are connected with the army. This is not surprising, for, to the Romans, Britain was a military problem.

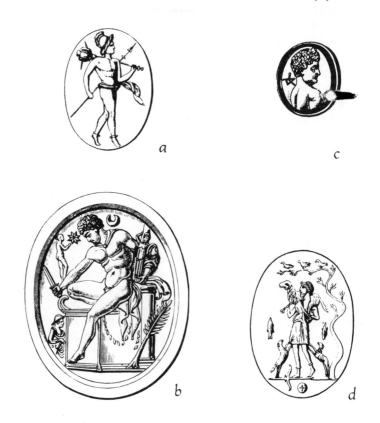

Fig. 9. Engraved gems, cut in intaglio. (a) Mars Gradivus. Red jasper from Charterhouse on Mendip, Somerset; second century A.D. (b) Diomedes climbing over the altar of Apollo at Troy in order to steal the Palladium. Onyx, in the Duke of Northumberland's collection at Alnwick Castle; findspot not known. ? First century A.D. (c) The Emperor Caracalla in the guise of Mercury. Red jasper from South Shields, Co. Durham; early third century A.D. (d) The Good Shepherd. Sard from Capua, now in Corpus Christi College, Cambridge; fourth century A.D.

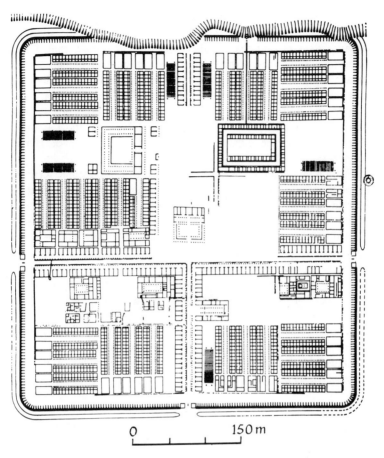

Fig. 10. Plan of the legionary fortress at Inchtuthil, Perthshire; first century A.D.

Indeed they thought it worth their while to retain three legions and many auxiliary regiments in the province.

The complete excavation of a first-century legionary fortress at Inchtuthil in Scotland (fig. 10) and the large number of small forts which have been examined (e.g. Hod Hill, Dorset and Housesteads, Northumberland) have added much to our understanding of the Roman army throughout the Empire.

There are of course important civil sites as well. The Palace at Fishbourne is surely one of the most significant Roman buildings in western Europe, not so much for the beauty of its mosaics (there are more impressive ones elsewhere in Britain) or for the fine garden now replanted with shrubs, or indeed for its state of preservation, but because its size and the details of its planning show that a most important person lived there. He was certainly an official (for the palace replaces a military base) and very probably the client-king Cogidubnus who is mentioned by Tacitus. The building is of similar size to the governor's palaces at London and Cologne and even holds its own with some of the Imperial palaces on the Palatine in Rome. Perhaps the closest comparison is with some of Herod's residences (e.g. the 'hanging palace' at Masada).

From a later period we have a fine villa at Lullingstone, Kent: the home of an administrator, proud of his ancestors (for he brought two marble busts with him, perhaps from Italy) and whose descendants – or at least successors as owners of the house – were converted to Christianity. At Lullingstone there was a church in the fourth century, with painted plaster walls that are immediately reminiscent of the house church excavated at Dura Europos on the Euphrates. The Lullingstone plaster is now in the British Museum. Here we have a glimpse of the Christianisation of the gentry which is one characteristic of the rich villa-culture of late Roman Britain and Gaul, a culture which reveals itself as much in the poetry of Ausonius and the letters of Sidonius Apollinaris as in the fine mosaics of Lullingstone, Woodchester, Hinton St Mary, Low Ham, Chedworth and Bignor.

Gaul

In Gaul (France, Belgium and part of Germany) there are rather different problems. The standard of excavation has seldom been as high as it is in Britain, but buildings are often much better preserved. The obvious crudities of much Romano-British sculpture, and the absence of triumphal arches and of lavishly decorated theatres in our country are more than compensated for by the remains of Roman Provence, the Republican 'Provincia' which had been conquered in the second century B.C. after having been influenced by the Greek city of Marseilles (Massilia) for over 300 years.

The Mausoleum of the Julii at St Remy has the lightness of the best Greek architecture; the character of the sculpture perhaps suggests that the workmen came from Asia Minor. The theatres at Vaison, Vienne and, above all, Orange, were built for an audience (Italian immigrants and Romanised provincials) which expected luxury. We should remind ourselves that the families of Agricola and Tacitus came from this very area. The triumphal arches of Orange and Carpentras show Gallic craftsmen working in a highly complicated classical style. The excellent example of southern Gaul was followed further north, as the theatre and Odeon (or Concert Hall) at Lyons, the beautiful gates of Autun, and the imposing baths at Paris bear witness.

The great days of Gaul came to an end in the third century, but no student of the later Roman Empire can afford to ignore the city of Trier, at several times in the third and fourth centuries an imperial capital. Its great gate, now known as the *Porta Nigra,* symbolises the sacred residence of the Emperors. Once inside the city it is not easy to miss the most important part of the Palatium, the audience chamber (*Aula Palatina*), which still survives, although its interior is now bare of fresco and mosaic (fig. 11). However, a series of fine ceiling paintings has come to light, depicting cupids and ladies of the Imperial House (perhaps Helena and Fausta, the mother and wife of Constantine). The paintings had fallen when part of the palace was destroyed to make way for the Cathedral, itself a magnificent building, which in its original form was larger than old St Peter's in Rome.

Cologne, an important *colonia* and centre of the glass industry, was capital of Lower Germany, and also preserves important Roman remains such as the governor's palace referred to above, a mosaic showing Bacchus and his *thiasos* (maenads and satyrs) and traces of various churches, of which St Severin is possibly the most notable.

Other Roman provinces

Spain has often been neglected by classical archaeologists, but spectacular aqueducts (Segovia and Tarragona) and bridges (e.g. the bridge over the Tagus at Alcantara) show better than anything the Roman skill in taming difficult country. There are also fine public buildings such as the theatres at Merida and Saguntum, the amphitheatre at Italica and the circus at Merida.

Tunisia and Western Libya (Tripolitania) are particularly full of fine town sites: in Roman times North Africa was a rich agricultural area devoted to the growing of corn and the olive, providing also wild animals from the hinterland for the amphitheatres of the west. It is easy to find Carthaginian influences in the buildings of Dugga, Mactar and Lepcis Magna. Tall, rather badly proportioned temples and over-ornate detailing annoy the purist but delight the Roman archaeologist attempting to seek for diversity within the Empire.

Local features also occur in the buildings of the Levant where the

Fig. 11

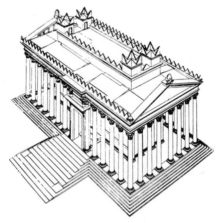

Fig. 12

Fig. 11. Reconstruction of the Aula Palatina, Trier; fourth century A.D.

Fig. 12. Reconstruction of the Temple of Bel, Palmyra; early first century A.D.

language of classical architecture had been familiar since early Hellenistic times. However, this architecture is combined with traditional forms to produce a greater diversity of effect than anywhere else in the Empire. Consider the Temple of the Sun at Baalbek which overpowers us by its size, the baroque curves of the colonnades at Jerash, and the illusionism of the rock-cut tombs at Petra and the elaborate decorative detail of some of the buildings at Palmyra (fig. 12). In the east archaeology is largely a matter of disengaging buildings from the sand and of understanding the influences which have dictated their style, although, naturally, excavation is sometimes useful. The town of Dura Europos is especially well understood after a long campaign of exploration conducted by Yale University.

Asia Minor and Greece are of exceptional interest for demonstrating the essential continuity of the ancient world.

It is hard to disentangle the sequence at many sites, and much of the masonry now visible at Ephesus, Olympia and Eleusis will belong to the Roman period, yet the Greek character of the various structures remains. Furthermore ancient buildings continued to be used: the Parthenon in Athens was as much a temple of Pallas Athena in the Roman period as in the fifth or fourth centuries B.C.

Nevertheless there is some original Roman architecture in the Balkans, for example Hadrian's library and gate at Athens and the mausoleum of Galerius (later the church of Haghios Giorgios) at Thessalonica.

Constantinople was founded by Constantine on the site of Greek Byzantium. Its surviving buildings are for the most part considerably later in date, but the Theodosian Wall, the best example of a town defence in the Empire, belongs to the century of the city's foundation.

The palace of Diocletian at Split in Jugoslavia, half a camp and half a place of retirement, expresses the moment when the emperor ceased to be a mere earthly ruler and became the viceregent of the gods (or, if he was a Christian, of God). It is strange and oriental; forbidding like a castle yet showing still the grace of refinement of classical architecture in its rational plan.

Italy

The essential qualities of Roman civilisation are best captured in Italy, the heart of the Empire. Rome has conserved, in part at least, a high proportion of the famous buildings which made her the wonder of the ancient world. In the second century Aelius Aristides wrote 'if one looks at the whole empire and reflects how small a fraction rules the whole world, he may be amazed at the city, but when he has beheld the city herself and the boundaries of the city, he can no longer be amazed that the entire civilized world is ruled by one so great' (*Orationes* XXXVI, 62). The layout of the Imperial *fora* or Trajan's market bear eloquent testimony to the love of order which distinguishes the Roman townscape from the Greek. The latter seldom took the same trouble to plan their cities as the Romans. Indeed, the typical *agora* is merely an open space surrounded by a jumble of buildings. At Ostia, the port of Rome, one can see how the Roman city is divided up into a grid of squares (*insulae*) occupied by apartment blocks or public buildings. The greatness of Roman architecture, in truth, lies not so much in its grandeur but in its sense of proportion. The compact houses of Pompeii and Herculaneum with their little colonnaded gardens and frescoed rooms better typify the Roman achievement than the imperial palaces of Hadrian (at Tivoli) or of Maximian (if Piazza Armerina, Sicily, *was* his residence), brilliant as these must have been in their heyday. Unfortunately public imagination has been aroused all too often by such vulgar buildings as the Colosseum in Rome, which was erected by the Flavians as an exercise in propaganda; less is heard of many more characteristic and well designed structures (for example the market at Pozzuoli, or the beautiful temples of Assisi and Pola or the temple of Vesta in the forum at Rome (fig. 13)) which still proclaim the old Hellenic adage, 'Nothing in excess'.

Fig. 13. Reconstruction of the Temple of Vesta, Rome; c. A.D. 200.

THE END OF ROME

In the Middle Ages men could not understand the true qualities of Roman architecture, which seemed to be the work of giants. Gradually from the time of the Renaissance, the rich human quality of the civilisation was rediscovered. There were bad features – slavery, the amphitheatre, occasional tyranny (aimed at senators and Christians), but good outweighed bad, and as Rutilius Namatianus observed in the early fifth century, by 'offering the conquered equal rights under her laws, Rome made a city out of what was once a world'.

Sidonius Apollinaris, bishop of Clermont, was still able to appeal to the Empire as an ideal although the Roman state had betrayed his part of Gaul to the barbarians. With great bitterness he wrote,

'Our freedom has been bartered for the security of others . . . is this our due reward for enduring want and fire and sword and pestilence . . . ? Was it for the prospect of this infamous peace, that we ripped the herbage from the cracks in our walls and took it away for food . . . ? Is it for these many signal proofs of our devotion that . . . we have now been abandoned?'

A similar sentiment appears in the British appeal to the central government in A.D. 446: 'To Agitius, thrice consul, the groans of the Britons . . . the barbarians drive us into the sea, the sea drives us to the barbarians: between these two means of death we are either killed or drowned.'

One has the feeling that the western Empire fell apart against both the will and the best interests of the governed. The myth of King Arthur, founded no doubt on a historical figure who defeated the Saxons in Britain around the year A.D. 500, could not have grown up anywhere else but in a sub-Roman milieu. Through the church and the continued survival of the eastern Empire the seeds of renewal were kept alive to germinate in unlikely places such as the monasteries of Ireland and Northumbria, in the seventh and eighth centuries. Latin remained the lingua franca of educated people in western Europe throughout the Middle Ages, and the diverse and complex society of the late antique aristocracy is mirrored in that of the Carolingian Court.

4

Medieval Europe

David Whitehouse

Medieval studies in Europe differ profoundly from the study of prehistory and significantly from the study of early civilisations. In every case, it is true, the archaeologist calls upon the same repertoire of field and laboratory techniques, but for medieval Europe (to an extent far greater than for classical antiquity) archaeology is often only one of several methods of enquiry, and for this reason we should begin by defining the scope of the chapter which follows.

First, the time span. Scholars argue about the event or events which mark the beginning of the Middle Ages. Some choose the adoption of Christianity by Constantine the Great in 312, others prefer the coronation of Charlemagne in the year 800; in Britain, many archaeologists restrict the term 'medieval' to the period after 1066. Throughout Europe, the *end* of the Middle Ages is taken to be some time in the fifteenth century. This 'epochal' approach, of course, is a matter of convenience rather than an accurate reflection of sudden fundamental change. Here, we are concerned with elements of continuity in medieval culture just as much as with elements of change. We shall begin with the migrations of the fourth and fifth centuries and end with the Norman states in the twelfth century, especially the kingdom of England.

Although this span embraces little more than half the duration of the British Neolithic and is immensely shorter than the Palaeolithic period, it is impossible to give a comprehensive review. The reason is simple: despite enormous gaps in the evidence, we know a vast amount about medieval Europe. Many aspects of life are documented in minute detail by a variety of sources. We know far more about the population of medieval Winchester than we shall ever know about Çatal Hüyük (see page 29) or the Palaeolithic inhabitants of the Terra Amata site (page 12). This chapter, therefore, is highly selective; it discusses a number of developments, each of which contributed towards the making of medieval Europe.

The medievalist has a wide range of potential sources of information. Frequently, he has a huge volume of documentary

80

evidence; in Britain, we have manuscripts of the seventh century, although large archives exist only for the twelfth century and later. He has archaeological evidence derived from the excavation and study of monuments, artefacts and plant and animal remains. He has the information provided by art and architectural historians, students of language and place-names, and by numismatists. Unfortunately, even today, scholars frequently concentrate on a single source of information, so that co-ordinated attempts to investigate a particular problem are the exception rather than the rule. This narrow approach is partly dictated by the nature of the evidence. In the course of the Middle Ages, Europe was occupied by a wide variety of cultures, and today each may be represented by a different range of artefacts, place-names and documents. Thus, the study of the Migration Period depends to a great extent on the excavation of cemeteries and an examination of the grave goods they contain. By contrast, we know little about the material culture of the Danes during their occupation of England, and scholars lean heavily on documents and place-name studies. Nevertheless, other periods are represented more fully and the medievalist will understand his subject only if he uses all the available sources. We should not think in terms of medieval history, archaeology or numismatics, but of medieval studies as a whole, and the notes which follow are based on the work of students in several specialist fields.

The end of the Roman Empire

Throughout Europe, the fourth and fifth centuries were a time of change. The Roman provinces, which had occupied much of temperate Europe, collapsed and were replaced by peasant communities with a different structure and technology. In the Mediterranean region, immigrants from the north and north-east settled in parts of Italy, Spain, North Africa and the Balkans. From the Roman point of view, the period was catastrophic (fig. 1).

The civilisation of Rome, as we saw in the previous chapter, developed in the Mediterranean basin, deriving much from the cultures of the Greeks and Etruscans. The Roman Empire was rooted in the Mediterranean. When expansion beyond the Alps became essential as a source of revenue, manpower, metals and other raw materials, the new provinces were outposts of a Mediterranean power. The largest cities – Antioch and Alexandria, for example – were in the Mediterranean, and the busiest trade routes were the sea lanes of the Mediterranean basin.

By the time of Roman expansion, the Mediterranean already had

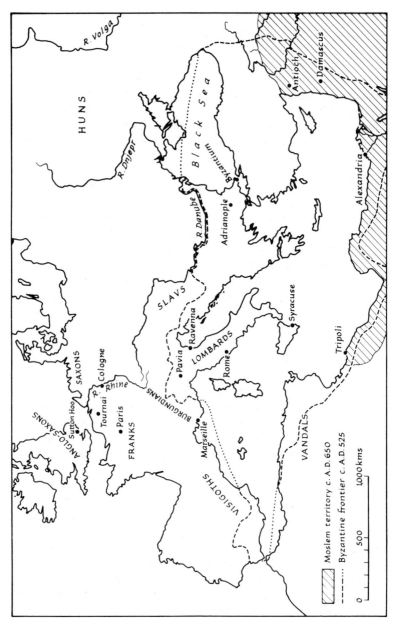

Fig. 1. *Europe between the fifth and the seventh centuries, show-ing the extent of the Byzantine Empire under Justinian c. 530, the extent of territory in Moslem hands c. 650 (shaded) and the location of 'barbarian' groups at the end of the Migration Period.*

a long history of urban civilisation, especially in the east. Temperate Europe, on the other hand, had no such tradition, and the expansion of Rome introduced the first truly urban society north of the Alps. Indeed, the Romans' first move when creating a new province was to establish towns. At the same time, other hallmarks of civilisation appeared: widely-based communications, a comprehensive monetary and fiscal system, ambitious civil engineering and literacy. By introducing these features, Roman expansion changed the face of Europe almost as dramatically as European expansion changed the face of the Americas, a millennium and a half later.

As the Empire declined, the frontiers were withdrawn towards the Mediterranean basin. Scholars have debated the decline of Rome for generations, citing a combination of causes: pressure from outside the north and eastern frontiers, massive inflation, and internal dissent provoked by the absence of a regular succession to power. In the Mediterranean, demographers point to a declining birth rate in the early centuries A.D., the resurgence of malaria and recurrent epidemics of plague. The most resilient parts of the Empire were the long-established cities of the east. After the failure of an attempt by Diocletian (284–305) to stem the decline by introducing sweeping political and monetary reforms, Constantine (emperor 306–36) realised that the process was irreversible; abandoning Rome, he established a new imperial capital in the east. The city he chose was Byzantium, now re-named Constantinople (330). It was a brilliant choice, for the city was to remain a capital for nearly sixteen centuries.

The Migration Period

The Migration Period, during which 'barbarian' peoples settled in many of the former provinces, thus began against the background of a declining Empire. The first cracks in the security of the outer provinces had appeared in the third century. In the North Sea, piracy became a serious problem and was countered with a fleet strong enough to enable its admiral, Carausius, to usurp power in 287. In Gaul, bands of disaffected peasants, or *bagaudae,* waged intermittent guerrilla warfare against the provincial administrations. Clearly, the provinces were already under pressure *before* the threat of invasion arose.

The threat did not come from an army. When the Romans advanced across the Alps, they did so with a professional military force. The new invaders were entirely different. They consisted of whole populations in search of a new place to live: hence the name

'Migration Period', which is now used in preference to the more emotive term 'the Dark Ages'.

The first invaders appeared in the east. Until the twentieth century, much of the Russian steppe was populated by nomadic or nearly-nomadic pastoralist communities. Mobility was a keynote of their existence, and movement by one group usually affected its neighbours. In the fourth century, movements on the western plains of Russia unsettled the Huns. To the south of them lived the Goths, a loose confederacy comprising the Ostrogoths in the Crimea and the Visigoths in the Danube basin. Agitated by the Huns, the Goths advanced across the Roman frontier. In 378 they defeated a Roman army at Adrianople (Edirne, on the modern border between Bulgaria and Turkey) and for a while threatened Constantinople itself. The threat was averted and the Ostrogoths moved on to Italy, where Alaric sacked Rome in 410, while the Visigoths migrated to Gaul and eventually to Spain. The last Roman Emperor in the west, Romulus Augustulus, was deposed by a Gothic ruler in 476.

Migrations also disrupted the north, although here the invaders were much less mobile than the horsemen from the steppes and their movements took a different form. They began with infiltration, piracy and raids. The Roman governors tried to protect their provinces by settling groups of barbarians inside the imperial frontiers and recruiting more and more barbarian mercenaries. In Britain, many – but by no means all – scholars have seen as evidence of barbarian soldiers and settlers the distinctive military equipment of the fourth century and the so-called Romano-Saxon pottery. Despite the policy of creating buffer zones against incursions from the north, the provinces of Britain, Germany and Gaul were steadily eroded in the fourth and fifth centuries. When the barriers finally broke, the Franks migrated from the Lower Rhine to Gaul, where in 482 Clovis became their first king, taking also the Roman title *consul*. After the Romans abandoned the provinces of Britain c. 408, England was invaded by groups of settlers from Denmark, Germany and the Low Countries, among whom the best known were the Angles, Saxons and Jutes.

The evidence for the course of the migrations into England consists of: (1) short and sometimes contradictory notes by such historians as Procopius and Bede, (2) archaeological material, and (3) place names and language. The archaeological evidence comes largely from cemeteries, although in recent years several important settlements have been examined, including the extensive site of Mucking on the Thames estuary. The invaders, who either buried or

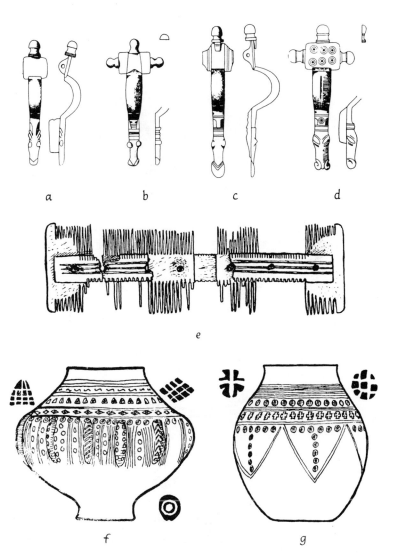

a b c d

e

f g

Fig. 2. Finds from cemeteries of the Migration Period in England: (a)–(d) bronze brooches from Sarre, Faversham, Howletts and Lyminge, all in Kent; (e) bone comb from Lackford in Suffolk; (f) and (g) pottery, also from Lackford.

85

more often cremated their dead, customarily placed jewellery and other items in the graves. Study of the pottery and other objects which accompanied the dead has enabled the archaeologist to recognise numerous regional and chronological variants (fig. 2). Thus, the pottery vessels known as *buckelurnen* have close continental parallels, while different types of jewellery occur mainly

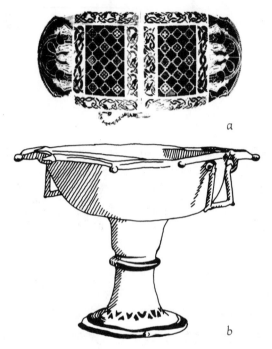

Fig. 3. Grave-goods from two outstanding Anglo-Saxon burials: (a) one of the pair of gold, garnet and glass mosaic clasps from Sutton Hoo and (b) a 'Coptic' bronze vessel, probably made in Egypt, found at Taplow in 1883.

in the East Midlands, the Thames valley or Kent. Many of these variants have been identified as the characteristic products of peoples mentioned in the documents. In this way, grave goods allow us to identify the cemeteries of the Angles in East Anglia, the East Midlands, Lincoln and Yorkshire, those of the Saxons in the Thames valley and parts of the south, and the Jutish cemeteries in Kent.

The invaders, who arrived mainly in the fifth century and consolidated their territory in the sixth, formed the bases of the several small kingdoms which existed in England by the time of Augustine's mission to Kent in 597. The prosperity of the ruling families is dramatically illustrated by rich burials, such as Taplow and Sutton Hoo (fig. 3). The latter yielded an astounding collection of grave goods, including a Byzantine silver dish, Frankish gold coins and sumptuous Anglo-Saxon jewellery, all placed in the cabin of a ship which was buried in a round barrow c. 640–50. In Northumberland, excavations at Yeavering have revealed the remains of a timber hall, an assembly place and other buildings identified as Gefrin, the royal residence where Paulinus preached to King Edwin in 627 (fig. 4).

By the end of the sixth century, when the Lombards moved into Italy and carved out two powerful duchies, large areas of the western Empire had been settled by peoples from outside the former frontiers. The long-term effects of the settlement depended on several variables, notably the size of the intrusive group and the strength of the Roman institutions they encountered. In Britain, the most 'provincial' of all the western provinces, most institutions were abandoned. Towns declined catastrophically and it appears that many – probably the majority – went out of use. The newcomers preferred their traditional economy based on small rural settlements with a high degree of self-sufficiency. In Gaul, on the other hand, the Franks moved into many of the Roman towns; they issued gold currency based on Roman models and adopted Roman titles. In Italy, Gothic rulers even dreamed of establishing their own imperial house. It was in Gaul, Italy and Spain that Latin survived, forming the basis of the modern Romance languages. Naturally enough the new vocabulary often recalled the 'vulgar' Latin of everyday speech, rather than the polite forms of the salon; the French *tête*, a head, is derived from Latin *testa,* a jar, rather than *caput,* while the Italian *cavallo,* a horse, is derived from *caballus,* a nag, rather than *equus,* the 'polite' word for a horse. Nevertheless, Latin survived, as it did in Vandal North Africa until the Moslem conquest of the seventh century.

The continuity of Mediterranean civilisation
Although in Italy, Spain and parts of North Africa the Lombards, Goths and Vandals adopted many Roman institutions, the greatest continuity was in the east. When Constantine transferred the capital to Byzantium, he moved to a city which occupied a strategic position, protected by the Sea of Marmora, the Bosporus and the Golden Horn, and controlling the trade route between the

87

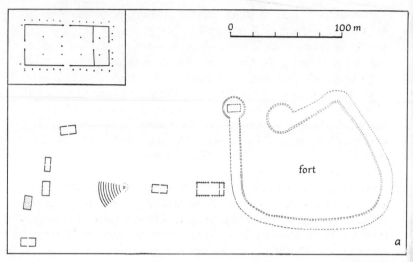

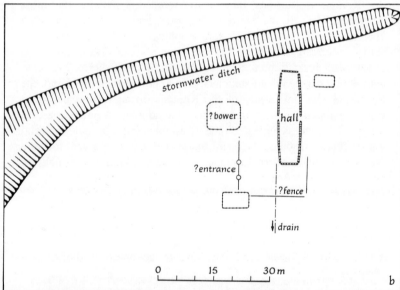

Fig. 4. Two Anglo-Saxon palaces: (a) Yeavering in the time of
Edwin (612-32) and (b) Cheddar in the time of Alfred the
Great (871-99).

88

Mediterranean and the Black Sea. Before the age of high explosives, Byzantium was almost impregnable; indeed, in the Middle Ages it was taken only once, by the Latins in 1204. The city grew rapidly and in the fifth century Theodosius II rebuilt the land walls, enclosing the recent suburbs. Under Justinian (527–65) the city received important new buildings, notably the metropolitan cathedral of Sancta Sophia. Gradually the character of the Byzantine Empire evolved, with a culture of (eastern) Hellenistic rather than (western) Roman origin and a distinct oriental flavour. The Emperor, for example, was attended by an elaborate court ritual reminiscent of the ritual which had shocked the Greeks so profoundly after Alexander's invasion of Persia, and 'Byzantine' became a byword for political complexity and intrigue. Despite the military disasters of the sixth and seventh centuries, in the course of which Arab armies occupied the provinces of Palestine, Syria and North Africa, the Byzantine Empire endured, providing western Europe with a source of luxury goods and influencing techniques and styles of ornament as far away as Scandinavia and Anglo-Saxon England. For centuries, merchants and mercenaries from north-west Europe knew Byzantium simply as *Mikelgaarde* – the Great City.

No comparable power emerged in the west Mediterranean until the eleventh century. True, the Visigoths in Spain and the Lombards in Italy established viable states, and urban life survived. Indeed, according to the distinguished historian Henri Pirenne (died 1935), for a while international trade also continued. In Pirenne's opinion, the turning point in the emergence of medieval Europe was not the flood of barbarian migrations but the expansion of Islam in the seventh century. Arab fleets, he maintained, commanded the Mediterranean, curbing the trade of the non-Moslem ports. This is an eccentric view and scholars have attacked it on almost every front. Nevertheless, the traditional urban economy did survive in Italy, southern France and parts of Spain, while among surviving institutions perhaps the most significant was the papacy. In time, the office of Bishop of Rome was transformed into that of a head of state. In the eighth century, Rome, although only a shadow of its former greatness, asserted its independence of Byzantium over the doctrinal issue of iconoclasm (which arose in 726) and in 800 the pope felt sufficiently confident to bestow the title Emperor on the Frankish king Charlemagne.

The conversion of western Europe

For more than four centuries Rome had fostered the institutions of urban civilisation in Europe north of the Alps. One of the Mediterranean features which accompanied the Romans was Christianity, and by the fourth century bishops existed in many of the cities of Gaul. Several towns in Britain, too, supported bishops, and archaeological finds indicate the presence of Christian communities and households. Silchester contained a building which may be a church, the villa at Hinton St Mary had an elaborate Christian mosaic, and a chapel existed in the villa at Lullingstone in Kent. When the Roman administration collapsed, Christianity was eclipsed; in Britain, the Anglo-Saxons introduced their own Teutonic pantheon. Christianity survived only in areas beyond the Anglo-Saxon settlements, and even here the majority of the population held pagan beliefs.

Christianity – the state religion throughout Europe at the end of the Middle Ages – was introduced in bursts of missionary activity from Byzantium and Rome. Ulfilas (c. 311–83), for example, led a mission to the Goths, using his own translation of the gospels into Gothic, a work which survives in part in the famous *Codex Argenteus* at Uppsala. The lasting importance of the conversion of barbarian Europe lies in the fact that the missions did not transmit religion alone; they also reintroduced literacy and a variety of Mediterranean crafts. Furthermore, by encouraging pilgrimage and establishing a network of monasteries they created new contacts between distant regions.

The first Anglo-Saxon mission was organised from Rome by Pope Gregory I (590–604). Its leader, Augustine, found a largely pagan country, although Christian communities existed in the Celtic west – in Cornwall, Wales, Ireland and in southern Scotland. Augustine made his headquarters at Canterbury: hence the special status of the Archbishop of Canterbury today. In 627 Paulinus led a mission to the north, preaching to Edwin of Northumbria at his palace of Yeavering. After 633, a major role in missionary activity in the north was played by the monks of Lindisfarne, a small island off the Northumbrian coast. Following the Synod of Whitby in 663, when differences between the Celtic and Roman churches were resolved, Theodore of Tarsus, Archbishop of Canterbury from 668 to 690, placed church organisation on a stable footing, although the country as a whole did not become even nominally Christian until generations later.

Thanks to the establishment of schools and *scriptoria* (studios of manuscript copyists) in the monasteries, learning and literacy were encouraged. Bede, writing at Jarrow, one of the centres of the

'Northumbrian Renaissance' of the late seventh century, produced his *Ecclesiastical History;* another Anglo-Saxon, Boniface, led a mission to Germany and became archbishop of Mainz; at the end of the eighth century Alcuin of York became a counsellor at Charlemagne's court.

Western Europe in the eighth and ninth centuries

During the eighth century, the small kingdoms which had emerged in the Migration Period gave way to larger political powers, each with a more cohesive social and administrative system than had existed previously. On the continent, Charlemagne (768–814) inherited half of the Frankish kingdom from his father Pepin III and transformed this into the nucleus of a powerful, if short-lived empire – in its day the largest political unit ever developed in Europe north of the Alps (fig. 5). Pepin had been a firm ally of the pope, and Charlemagne continued this policy. In 773, responding to an appeal by the pope for aid against the Lombard king Didier, Charlemagne laid siege to the Lombard capital, Pavia. When the city surrendered in 774, Charlemagne assumed the title *Rex Longobardorum* and became an important personality in Mediterranean politics. In 800, under circumstances which have never been explained satisfactorily, Charlemagne was crowned Emperor of the West by Pope Leo III.

The most far-reaching effect of Charlemagne's Italian ventures was his conscious attempt to re-establish Mediterranean culture north of the Alps. This *renovatio,* or renewal, began after the conquest of Lombardy. In 794, Charlemagne abandoned the traditional practice whereby Frankish kings progressed through their territory, and selected instead a permanent capital, Aachen, after the example of Mediterranean capitals like Rome or Pavia. Aachen became the focal point of the cultural revival. The Palatine Chapel (probably dedicated in 805) was built along the lines of a Mediterranean church, recalling San Vitale at Ravenna (fig. 6). Elsewhere, the Oratory of Theodulf at Germigny-des-Prés (dedicated in 806) was decorated with mosaics of Byzantine type, while the great Abbey Church at Fulda (consecrated in 819) resembled the Basilica of St Peter at Rome.

At the same time, Charlemagne fostered a literary revival, surpassing the efforts of all but the largest monastic scriptoria already in existence. Scholars like Alcuin and the Lombard historian Paul the Deacon were imported from Anglo-Saxon England and Italy. Latin texts were copied and distributed with renewed vigour and manuscript illumination in the new court style flourished. By the

91

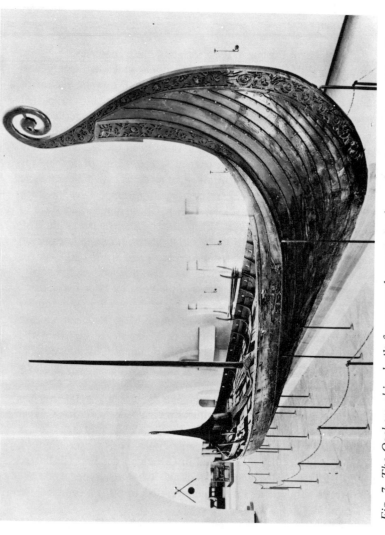

Fig. 7. The Oseberg ship, built for coastal waters in the early ninth century. The ship, which was propelled by thirty oarsmen and a sail, is 21.5 metres long.

mid-ninth century, a new level of culture had been established, out of which developed much of the art of western Europe in the years which followed.

Meanwhile, in England, more prosaic but no less important developments were taking place. The first partial unification of the country was achieved by Offa, king of Mercia (757–96). Offa first annexed the kingdoms of East Anglia and Essex. Later, he gained control of Wessex, Sussex and the Isle of Wight and in 670 felt justified in proclaiming himself *Rex totius Anglorum patriae,* King of All England. Among the reforms instigated by Offa was the reorganisation of the English currency, during which the silver *sceatta* was replaced by the penny. The growing need for an efficient monetary system presupposes regular trade and the germ of an urban economy; evidently, the developments which took place under Alfred and his successors had their origin in the eighth century reforms of Offa.

Towns and trade

When the Romans withdrew from the northern provinces, urban life declined. The system suffered most in Britain, where the Anglo-Saxons introduced an economy and society in which towns were virtually irrelevant. Although recent excavations at Canterbury (Durovernum), St Albans (Verulamium) and other sites have shown that some towns were still occupied in the fifth century, they confirm that none survived on its former scale and many disappeared completely. On the continent, especially in southern France, the majority survived, although here again the scale of urban activity decreased in every region. It was not until the ninth century that towns and a market economy re-appeared over large areas of Europe north of the Alps.

In the Mediterranean basin the situation was different. In the east, urban civilisation continued, both in Byzantine territory and in the regions conquered by the Moslems in the seventh century. In the west, towns and trade declined, partly as a result of the barbarian migrations and partly under the impact of the Islamic armies which overran much of the Mediterranean basin. The Moslems had acquired most of North Africa (including the Maghrib) by 698. They invaded Spain in 711 and in the ninth century they occupied Sicily. However, Moslem traders ensured the prosperity of towns in North Africa (notably Qairawan) and Spain, while in Italy Naples, Amalfi, Bari and Venice all became wealthy ports. The will of Justinian Partecipazio, Doge of Venice, in 829 shows that he invested in

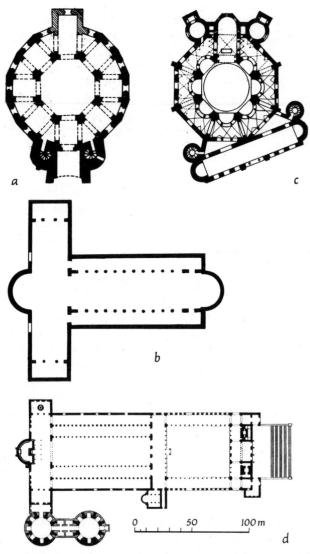

Fig. 6. The Carolingian Renewal. Plans of (a) the Palatine Chapel, Aachen (consecrated c. 805) and (b) the Abbey Church, Fulda (consecrated in 819) with their Mediterranean prototypes: (c) San Vitale, Ravenna (consecrated in 547) and (d) the Basilica of St Peter, Rome, built by Constantine the Great. Note: Old St Peter's was demolished in 1505 and the plan is restored.

94

market trade, and by the tenth century Venice dominated Italian commerce. The Golden Bull of 992 confirmed Venetian supremacy over competitors farther afield, and in 1082 the Emperor Alexius I granted Venetian merchants freedom of trade throughout the Byzantine Empire.

Medieval towns depended for their existence on market trade. Food and raw materials were purchased from adjacent communities and paid for from the profits of trade. In north-west Europe, trade was of minor importance until the eighth and ninth centuries, when economic expansion on both sides of the North Sea and the English Channel led to the rise of ports like Quentovic, Duurstede and Hamwih (Southampton). At the same time, towns came into existence at strategic points on rivers and cross-country routes. In the archaeological record, the international activities of merchants in the ninth and tenth centuries are well illustrated by the distribution on both sides of the North Sea of Badorf ware amphorae and Pingsdorf ware wine jars, exported from the Middle Rhine, presumably filled with wine.

In England, Alfred and his immediate successors established *burgs,* or fortified towns, with a regular grid of streets. The burgs were commercial and administrative centres, usually accommodating both markets and mints, which supplied the rigidly-controlled silver currency of late Saxon England. In the countryside, a timber palace occupied during the reign of Alfred has been excavated at Cheddar in Somerset (fig. 4b), and elsewhere in England later Saxon buildings are coming to light in steadily increasing numbers.

The development of the town in medieval Europe has long interested the economic historian, and in recent years it has attracted the attention of the archaeologist. Whenever possible, documentary research, study of the surviving monuments, excavation and place-name studies are combined in an attempt to elucidate the changing form and function of the town. In Britain, the largest excavation so far is at Winchester, where the Research Unit, directed by Martin Biddle, has excavated the Anglo-Saxon minster, a Norman and later palace, the castle and an area containing workshops and a church. Other excavations include Thetford (part of the Anglo-Saxon town), Stamford, Southampton and Norwich. Lately, the pace of research has quickened as redevelopment obliterates large areas of existing towns. Indeed, one of the primary objectives of the organisation *Rescue* is – literally – to rescue evidence before it is destroyed.

Elsewhere in Europe, the outstanding excavation of a medieval

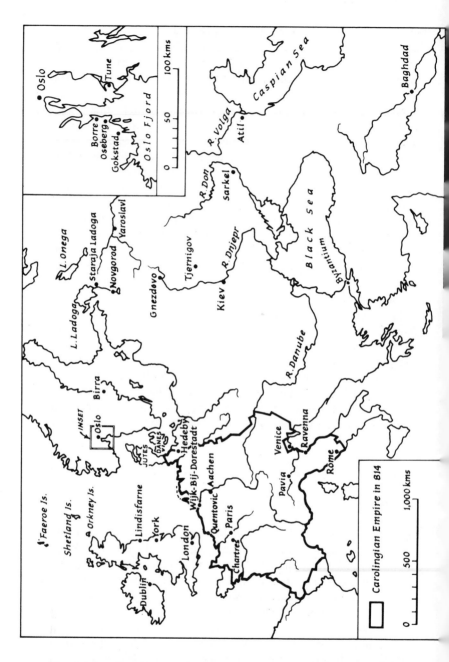

Fig. 5. The Carolingian Empire at the death of Charlemagne in 814, also illustrating Viking activity c. 800-1050. The inset shows Oslo Fjord and the sites of important Viking burials.

city is the work of Artiskhovsky and Kolchin at Novgorod, 160 kilometres south of Leningrad. The most important campaigns at Novgorod took place between 1951 and 62, during which the excavators uncovered more than a thousand timber buildings, associated with streets of split tree trunks forming corduroys 4–5 metres wide. The streets were renewed repeatedly and in all some twenty-eight surfaces were found, spanning the period from c. 950 until the fifteenth century. In the moist soil conditions the timbers of both buildings and streets survived to a remarkable extent, as did other perishable objects, such as documents written on birch bark, wooden vessels and leather.

The Vikings

Meanwhile, a new power was developing in the north. For three centuries, beginning about 780, the Vikings of Scandinavia were a major force in Europe. The Vikings did not belong to a single ethnic or cultural group and they never united as a single state. Nevertheless, Viking activities conform to a pattern, whether they were mounted from Denmark, Norway or Sweden, and it is possible to discuss them together (fig. 5).

The Vikings impressed their contemporaries first as raiders. Beginning at the end of the eighth century, they carried out a series of violent coastal raids on the Low Countries, France and the British Isles. The *Anglo-Saxon Chronicle* records a long list of attacks, commencing with raids in 789 and 793, when Vikings destroyed the monastery of Lindisfarne. In the ninth century, the intensity of the raids increased and some of the wealthiest North Sea ports were destroyed; Duurstede fell in 834, Quentovic in 842.

Piracy, however, was only one aspect of Viking activity and it was as settlers and traders that the Vikings made their most lasting contribution to medieval Europe. Overpopulation at home compelled settlers to explore the Atlantic coasts to the south and west, while a desire for commerce led others to open up profitable trade routes between the Baltic and western Asia. Sophisticated ships, exemplified by the vessels interred with the rich burials at Gokstad, Oseberg and Tune (fig. 7), enabled the Vikings to investigate regions which hitherto had lain beyond the reach of European sailors.

Expeditions of Viking settlers began to force their way into the coastal areas of western Europe in the ninth century. Norwegian settlers had established a kingdom in Ireland, based on Dublin, by the 850s while, in England, the Danes made their headquarters at York in 867. Following this early success, the Danes mounted a determined invasion of England. After attacking Mercia, they advanced into East Anglia in 869 and into Wessex a year later. By 874 Mercia had collapsed and in 877 its eastern counties were divided among Danish settlers. Two years later the Danes settled in East Anglia. Thus, by 879 a large part of eastern England contained Danish settlers and in the eleventh century the region was still known as the *Danelaw* – the area in which Danish laws and customs prevailed. Wessex, thanks largely to the efforts of Alfred, survived these Viking incursions and made an acceptable peace with the Danes in 878. Although the material evidence for Danish settlement is slight, its extent is illustrated vividly by the distribution of place-names containing Danish elements, such as the suffixes *-by* (as in Derby) and *-thorpe* (as in Scunthorpe).

Viking expansion into the remote parts of the North Atlantic followed a different pattern. Compared with western Europe, the Faeroes, Iceland and Greenland were sparsely populated and consequently Viking settlement took a more peaceful course. The Vikings reached the Faeroes about 800, a century after the reputed dicovery of the islands by anchorite priests from Ireland. The Irish also discovered Iceland and about 860 the first Viking settlers began to explore the island. By c. 930 Vikings (mostly from Norway) occupied all the habitable areas, where they lived by farming, fishing and hunting seal. However, the most famous voyages were those which led to the discovery of Greenland and North America. The Viking sagas tell us that Greenland was discovered in 982 and five years later an expedition of twenty-five ships brought the first settlers from Iceland. The Vikings planted colonies along the south and west coasts, and archaeologists have found the sites of numerous farms and settlements. Meanwhile, in 986, the first European vessel, commanded by Bjarni Herjolfsson, probably reached America. We are told that during the next forty years a series of voyages by raiders and would-be settlers met with indifferent success and, after a skirmish with the local population, attempts to colonise the coast of North America were abandoned.

Although the Vikings traded in the west, it was in eastern Europe and Asia that they enjoyed their greatest commercial success. During the ninth century, Scandinavians established a trade route through Russia to the Black Sea and, according to the so-called *Nestorian Chronicle,* they played a key role in establishing the city states of Novgorod and Kiev. Merchants sailed from Baltic ports, such as Hedeby, to the Gulf of Finland. Thence they travelled overland to Lake Ladoga, Novgorod and Smolensk. Here they reached the River Dnjepr, which they then followed to Kiev and the Black Sea. Their most frequent destination was Byzantium, where Scandinavians had trading rights and formèd part of the Imperial Varangian Guard. An alternative route took them farther east, via the Volga, to the Caspian Sea, whence caravan routes led eastwards to Chorezm and the central Asian cities of Bukhara and Samarkand, or south to Baghdad. In Scandinavia thousands of Islamic silver coins attest to the volume of trade, while isolated finds of Viking artefacts in the east (such as the runic inscription from Berezany on the Black Sea) illustrate the movements of individual merchants and soldiers of fortune.

The Normans

While Viking adventurers explored the North Atlantic and forged links with Byzantium and the east, a new Viking state was emerging in western Europe: Normandy.

The origins of Normandy go back to the early tenth century. In 911 the Danish or Norwegian Viking Hrolf (known as Rollo in the French sources) attacked the French coast and penetrated inland as far as Chartres. Although defeated by the Franks, the Vikings were allowed to settle in the Seine valley west of Rouen, the capital of the Frankish province of Neustria. From the Frankish point of view, their policy of appeasement was short-sighted, and by 918 the Vikings had expanded their territory and captured Rouen. Six years later they had pushed their frontiers even farther inland, and in 932 Duke William I advanced to the River Couesnon, which remained the effective boundary of Normandy throughout the Middle Ages. Indeed, by the middle of the tenth century, the Duchy of Normandy had attained its full extent.

The Vikings, or Normans (i.e. men from the north) as the Franks called them, did not replace the local population, and Norman culture soon assimilated many Frankish customs. The Normans retained Rouen as the principal town. Under Duke Richard I they adopted Christianity as the official religion and with it the close relationship between church and state which had been current among the Franks since the reign of Charlemagne. They adopted the French language; the very title *Duke* was a Frankish usage.

In the mid-eleventh century, the Normans acquired two foreign kingdoms: England and Sicily. They arrived in Italy as mercenary soldiers, fighting first for the Lombards against the Byzantines in 1017 and later for the Byzantines against the Moslems in 1038 and

40. The Normans demanded land in return for their services and in 1037 they were confirmed in possession of Aversa near Naples. The nature of the Normans' activities changed in 1040, with the arrival in Italy of Guillaume d'Hauteville. Under his command, a group of Norman mercenaries seized the Byzantine town of Melfi in 1041. Guillaume assumed the title Count of Apulia and rapidly extended the Norman territory to include much of southern Italy. In 1047 Guillaume's younger brother, Robert Guiscard came to Italy and began to ravage Calabria. By 1060 the south was in Norman hands, and the following year Guiscard invaded Sicily. Palermo fell in 1072, and by the end of the century the island had been completely subdued. Under the Normans Sicily prospered, with a multiracial society in which Greek, Moslem, Italian and Norman elements existed side by side.

The conquest of England followed a different pattern. The Anglo-Saxons had been in close contact with Normandy since 991, when the Treaty of Rouen affirmed that neither state would help the enemies of the other. The connection was strengthened by marriages between the ruling families and, when Cnut the Dane invaded Wessex in 1013, members of the royal house took refuge in Normandy. Under Edward the Confessor (1043–66) the English maintained their alliance, and contemporary sources, including the *Anglo-Saxon Chronicle,* claim that Edward nominated Duke William II (William the Conqueror) to succeed him as king of England. In 1064 William had consolidated his position by compelling Harold, the son of Godwine, Earl of Wessex and the obvious English choice as successor, to swear an oath of allegiance. The Norman chroniclers and the designer of the eleventh century Bayeux Tapestry agree that, by 1066, William had established a strong claim to the English throne.

Plans for a Norman invasion followed swiftly on the news that Harold had been acclaimed King on Edward's death. The Channel crossing was perhaps the most ambitious naval operation in western Europe since the withdrawal of the Roman fleets. Ten thousand soldiers, with cavalry and full equipment (including prefabricated towers) were landed by night at Pevensey. The invaders were met near Hastings by an English army which, although superior in numbers, was exhausted after forced marches to and from Yorkshire to repel a second invasion, from Scandinavia. Exhaustion apart, two factors decided the battle in the Normans' favour: their cavalry and their archers. Anglo-Saxon armies fought hand to hand: they possessed no organised cavalry and at Hastings Harold mustered only a handful of bowmen. At the end of the day, Harold was dead and the English were in flight.

William had assembled his army from forces raised by the Norman aristocracy, in return for which he had promised grants of English land, should the invasion succeed. Consequently, in the years following 1066, the old Anglo-Saxon estates were divided among the new Norman magnates. According to 'Domesday Book' – a thorough survey of property and goods and services owed to the king by his feudal landlords – William granted demesnes to some three hundred tenants in chief, while a total of approximately 1,500 received some form of grant. The greatest magnates, like Roger of Montgomery, acquired enormous holdings, with estates in several counties. If each recipient of land brought to England his family and servants, the Norman influx still cannot have exceeded 10,000. A sober estimate of the total population of England at the time of the Domesday survey is about 1·5 million, so that the Norman element accounted for less than 1 per cent of the inhabitants of the country. For this reason, rapid changes in the basic way of life, such as took place in the Migration Period, did not occur.

Nevertheless, the new aristocracy did introduce important innovations. The feudal system, which defined the status and obligations of all classes of society, was imposed in a more rigid form than had existed under the Anglo-Saxon kings. The state embarked on an ambitious programme of building, which established a new architectural style, the Norman version of Romanesque. Although the style began to influence England before the Conquest, it did not take hold until the later eleventh century. Using ashlar masonry, the Normans built on an impressive scale; their churches had wide vaulted roofs, massive piers and imposing façades flanked by towers. The style, which the Normans derived largely from Burgundy, is exemplified by the Abbey Church of St Etienne, Caen (begun c. 1067) and by the cathedrals of Peterborough, St Albans and Durham (begun in 1093). In the intellectual field, the church received new impetus under the influence of personalities such as Lanfranc, the Italian whom William installed as Archbishop of Canterbury in 1070. The army introduced a new strategy and developed a new element in power politics – the castle. In the programme of consolidation which followed the Conquest, earth and timber castles were built in every important town. Essentially the motte and bailey castles (fig. 8) consisted of a conical earthen mound (the motte) surmounted by a timber tower, with one or more fortified enclosures (baileys) to

101

contain outbuildings and to serve as a refuge in times of danger. During the twelfth century many of the timber castles were rebuilt in stone. Finally, French became the language of the court. In the upper echelons of society, English culture underwent a sudden and important change.

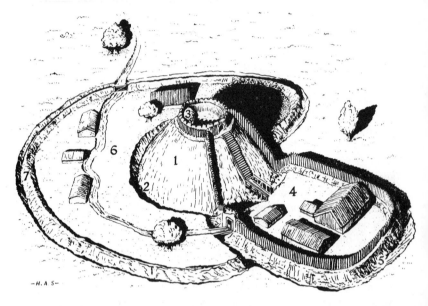

Fig. 8. The elements of a motte-and-bailey castle: (1) the motte, surrounded by (2) a ditch and surmounted by (3) a tower or keep; (4) the inner bailey, defended by (5) a ditch, bank and stockade; (6) the outer bailey, also protected by (7) a bank and ditch.

Town and country in Norman England

In the preceding paragraphs, I described aspects of medieval Europe before the twelfth century, notably the emergence of powerful states, such as the Carolingian Empire, north of the Alps and the re-establishment of towns and international trade. This concluding section discusses the characteristics of one small area – England – at the close of the period under review and contrasts them with the situation today.

Despite far-reaching changes, western Europe in the eleventh and twelfth centuries preserved the rural aspect it possessed in the Roman period and was, indeed, to retain until the Industrial

Revolution. Thus, the most striking features of Norman England were the small population and the uncultivated appearance of the countryside. The Domesday survey indicates that the total population was barely 1.5 million. The towns were small; London apparently contained only 10,000 inhabitants; Lincoln, Norwich and York each contained 6,000–7,000; Ipswich, Oxford and Thetford had about 5,000 each. In short, the combined populations of the *seven largest* towns in the kingdom numbered only 45,000 – the population of *one small* country town today.

Although the population had soared to an estimated 3.7 million in 1340 (on the eve of the Black Death), throughout the Middle Ages England, like most of Europe, was essentially rural, and the great majority of the population (more than 90 per cent at the time of the Domesday survey) lived on the land. In the country, most people lived in villages. Each village was largely self-sufficient and, as communications were poor, they were usually more self-contained than all but the most isolated rural communities today. The small size of the urban population meant that rural areas were not compelled to produce the large surpluses of meat and vegetables essential today, and consequently the areas of arable and regular grazing were relatively small. Beyond the fields and pastures of the village lay large tracts of waste ground – a valuable source of small game and innumerable herbs and wild fruit – and forest. Even in the Norman period, some of the woodland (in the Midlands, for example) may have been primary forest. Indeed, the *quantity* of timber presented a strong contrast to the situation today; one-fifth of the country consisted of forested royal preserves and the countryside as a whole had a tree-covered and little-used appearance.

Nevertheless, villages abounded and most present-day towns already existed at the time of the Norman conquest. The villages were small, often with a population of fewer than a hundred. A typical village might consist of a manor, church and the cottages of the landlord's tenants. Brick-making had ceased in England at the end of the Roman period and was not reintroduced until the thirteenth century; hence, in most lowland regions, peasant houses were built with a timber frame and panels of wattle and daub, a form of construction which survived in some areas until the last century. Although many churches were still built of timber, a growing proportion was now built in stone. Shops as we know them existed only in the towns. The village was surrounded by arable land, divided into small holdings and farmed in rotation to preserve the fertility of the soil. Animals were pastured in adjacent water meadows or scrub. Bread was the staple diet and within reach of most villages was a watermill for grinding flour.

The country was administered along feudal lines: a rigid pyramid of authority with the king at the top and the peasants at the bottom. Each village was administered by a feudal landlord (the lord of the manor), to whom the villagers rendered goods and services in return for personal security. Each landlord was bound to provide goods and services for a baron, perhaps a great landowner like Roger of Montgomery, who in turn owed allegiance to the king.

Although a wide variety of industrial techniques were known and practised, large factory complexes did not exist. In England, the nearest approaches to intensive industry were the mining settlements of the Weald and the Forest of Dean (iron), or the Mendips and Derbyshire (lead and silver). Other 'industrial' centres included the weaving villages and the salt towns, like Droitwich, whose merchants exported salt all over the Midlands and the Thames valley. Generally speaking, however, in the eleventh and twelfth centuries industry was conducted on a modest scale and usually was geared to serve the local consumer. Most potteries, for example, were small cottage industries employing only a handful of men.

When goods were produced for wider consumption, they were marketed in the towns. Each town was the focal point of its region and the right to hold a regular market encouraged prosperity and growth. On a still wider scale, the coastal towns of East Anglia and the English Channel profited from maritime trade with the Low Countries (e.g. Kings Lynn) and with Normandy and, later, Aquitaine (e.g. Southampton). With the establishment in 1066 of unified rule on both sides of the Channel, the tempo of trade and travel increased, so that continental habits and techniques, such as Gothic building construction using the groined vault and pointed arch, were readily introduced and rapidly diffused. In every way, England was now more closely connected with the continent than at any time since the Romans withdrew.

Select Bibliography

Chapter 1

A. The best book covering the environmental and geological background to man's evolution is Karl Butzer's *Environment and archaeology* (London 1971), but R. G. West's *Pleistocene geology and biology* (London 1968) and Kenneth Oakley's *Frameworks for dating fossil man* (London 1969) supplement it in different ways. The main points of view on human evolution can be found in C. L. Brace's *The stages of human evolution* (Englewood Cliffs 1967), John Napier's *The roots of mankind* (London 1971) and David Pilbeam's *The evolution of man* (London 1970); but the standard work is still probably T. Dobzhansky's *Mankind evolving* (Yale 1963). Perhaps the most useful texts on palaeolithic archaeology are F. Bordes' *The old stone age* (London 1968) which has a French slant, and John Wymer's *Lower Palaeolithic archaeology in Britain* (London 1968) with a British slant. There are many books on cave art. Peter Ucko and Andrée Rosenfeld's *Palaeolithic cave art* (London 1967) is the most easily available, A. Leroi-Gourhan's *The art of prehistoric man in western Europe* (London 1968) is the best illustrated, and S. Giedion's *The eternal present* (Oxford 1963) is the most thoughtful and provocative.

B. A more detailed account of the problems of neoteny raised in the text is Sir Gavin de Beer's *Embryos and ancestors* (Oxford 1950), and the classic view of Neanderthal extinction is H. Vallois' 'Neanderthals and Praesapiens' (*Journal of the Roy. Anth. Inst.* (1954) 84:111). The best book on the controversial problems of human fossil classification is the symposium edited by S. Washburn *Classification and human evolution* (London 1963). Different attitudes to earlier Palaeolithic man and his culture are F. Clark Howell's *European and northwest African Middle Pleistocene hominids* (Current Anthropology (Chicago, 1960) 1:195) and Desmond Collins' *Culture traditions and environment of early man* (CA (1969) 10:267), both wide ranging in scope. The special reports on various aspects of the Swanscombe skull and its context are edited by C. Ovey *The Swanscombe skull* (Roy. Anth. Inst. 1964). The remarkable new work done in southern France is partly available in H. de Lumley's 'A Palaeolithic camp at Nice' (*Scientific American* May 1969) or the more detailed 2 volume monograph *Le Paléolithique Inférieur du Midi Mediterranéen* (Paris 1969–71). Two detailed studies of the later Palaeolithic are P. A. Mellars' 'The chronology of the Mousterian industries in the Périgord region' (*Proceedings of the Prehistoric Soc. for 1969* 35:134, London 1970) and Hallam L. Movius' *Radiocarbon dates and Upper Palaeolithic archaeology in central and western Europe* (CA (1960) 1:355). The standard work on the British Upper Palaeolithic, D. A. E. Garrod's *Upper Palaeolithic age in Britain* (Oxford 1926) is now very out of date. J. G. D. Clark's *Star Carr* (Cambridge 1954) and *Star Carr: a case study in bioarchaeology* (Reading, Mass. 1972) may be consulted on this important mesolithic site.

Chapter 2

A. The following books provide a general account of the prehistory of Europe. They are all now out of date in some respects, but provide much basic background information. The work of V. Gordon Childe, though permeated by a diffusionist mode of thought that is now unfashionable, has to a very large degree formed our present understanding of European prehistory. Its importance can hardly be overestimated.

Childe, V. G. *Man makes himself* (London 1936: 4th edition 1965).
   New light on the most ancient east (London 1954).
   The dawn of European civilisation (6th edition London 1957).
   The Prehistory of European Society (London 1958).
Clark, J. G. D. *Prehistoric Europe. The economic basis* (London 1952).
Clark, G. and Piggott, S. *Prehistoric societies* (London 1965).
Piggott, S. *Ancient Europe* (Edinburgh 1965).

B. The following provide more detailed information on topics discussed particularly in the text. The two symposia (Braidwood and Willey 1962 and Ucko and Dimbleby 1969) contain several papers of relevance to the development of food-producing and later urban societies. Renfrew's recent book (1972) is the first detailed analysis of the local evolution of a civilisation through the framework of a systems model; its publication is likely to represent a turning point in the study of European prehistory. The other books and articles quoted refer to smaller topics and problems highlighted in the text.

Braidwood, R. J. and Willey, G. R. eds. *Courses toward urban life* (Edinburgh 1962).

Deevey, E. S. 'The Human Population.' *Scientific American* (1960).

Lamberg-Karlovsky, C. C. 'Mesopotamia and the Indo-Iranian Borderlands.' *Iran* X (1972).

Masson, V. M. 'The urban revolution in southern Turkmenia.' *Antiquity* XLII (1968).

Mellaart, J. *Çatal Hüyük* (London 1967).

Neustupny, E. 'A new epoch in radiocarbon dating.' *Antiquity* XLIV (1970).

Renfrew, C. 'The autonomy of the south-east European Copper Age.' *Proceedings of the Prehistoric Society* N.S. XXXV (1969).

Renfrew, C. *The emergence of civilisation. The Cyclades and the Aegean in the third millennium B.C.* (London 1972).

Thom, A. *Megalithic sites in Britain* (Oxford 1967).

Ucko, P. J. and Dimbleby, G. W. eds. *The domestication and exploitation of plants and animals* (London 1969).

Chapter 3

A. For the Greek 'background, the most lucid general account is perhaps C. M. Bowra's *The Greek experience* (London 1957). For the workings of Athenian democracy see A. E. Zimmern, *The Greek Commonwealth* (5th edition Oxford 1931). There is no outstanding work on the Hellenistic Age, but W. W. Tarn and G. T. Griffith's *Hellenistic civilisation* (3rd edition London 1952) is a competent summary. Naturally much has been written about Greek art, but the beginner could not do better than to consult John Boardman's concise survey *Greek Art* (London 1964).

For the Roman Republic, the historical and archaeological essay by A. H. McDonald (*Republican Rome* (London 1966)), is hardly to be surpassed. Michael Grant continues the story until the third century in his *The world of Rome* (London 1960) and *The climax of Rome* (London 1968). Peter Brown's *The world of Late Antiquity* (London 1971) is an admirable account of the transmutation of the Classical world into that of the early Middle Ages.

B. There are, of course, many more specialised works dealing with various aspects of Roman archaeology. On daily life, J. P. V. D. Balsdon, *Life and leisure in Ancient Rome* (London 1969) is a mine of information, some of it from very diverse sources. Graham Webster's *The Roman Imperial Army* (London 1969) provides a clear survey of a very important institution. The diverse religions of the Empire are well discussed by John Ferguson, *The religions of the Roman Empire* (London 1970). R. E. Witt, *Isis in the Graeco-Roman world* (London 1971) is an outstanding study of one of the most significant of the mystery cults, and A. D. Nock's classic *Conversion* (Oxford 1933) examines the background to the rise of Christianity in the Roman Empire. J. M. C. Toynbee, *Death and burial in the Roman world* (London 1971) can also be highly recommended. The same author's *The art of the Romans* (London 1965) is excellent on sculpture and painting and A. Boëthius and J. B. Ward-Perkins' *Etruscan and Roman architecture* (Harmondsworth 1970) is the ideal guide to building in the Empire. On coinage see Richard Reece, *Roman coins* (London 1970): this almost deserves a place in the first part of our bibliography, for as well as surveying the issues of the various mints, Mr Reece provides the sort of lucid political history of Rome necessary if we are to appreciate the significance of the Roman coin series. For Roman Britain, Sheppard Frere's *Britannia* (London 1967) supersedes earlier accounts of the province's history while R. G. Collingwood and I. A. Richmond, *The archaeology of Roman Britain* (2nd edition London 1969) is a comprehensive survey of the material remains. R. G. Collingwood and R. P. Wright, *The Roman inscriptions of Britain* I (Oxford 1965), abbreviated *RIB,* and J. M. C. Toynbee, *Art in Britain under the Romans* (Oxford 1964) are essential textbooks. Barry Cunliffe's *Fishbourne: a Roman palace and its garden* (London 1971) and Roger Goodburn's *Chedworth Roman Villa* (London, National Trust 1972) may also be mentioned. Amongst studies of individual cities in Britain, Ralph Merrifield's *Roman London* (London 1969) is outstanding. New discoveries are reported in the journal *Britannia* published by the Society for the Promotion of Roman Studies.

Books dealing with other provinces tend to be in foreign languages but we are fortunate to have in English, Olwen Brogan's *Roman Gaul* (London 1953) and Edith Wightman's *Roman Trier and the Treveri* (London 1970).

In addition to all the books mentioned, translations of numerous Greek and Roman authors are available in the Loeb Classical Library and Penguin Classics. What better introduction could there be to the Roman world than a civilised and humane historian such as Tacitus?

Chapter 4

A. The following provide an introduction to the history of medieval Europe. Lopez' book is an ambitious and abundantly illustrated account of the principal economic developments, while Loyn gives an excellent introduction to the Anglo-Saxon kingdoms and the impact of the Norman invasion.

Davis, H. W. C. *Medieval Europe* (2nd edition London 1960).
Lopez, R. S. *The birth of Europe* (London 1967).
Loyn, H. R. *Anglo-Saxon England and the Norman Conquest* (London 1962).
Southern, R. W. *The making of the Middle Ages* (London 1953).

B. The following provide more detailed information on particular topics. Bloch's *Feudal Society* is a classic study of a difficult and much-debated subject. Brown's short book is a brilliant account of the continuity of Mediterranean civilisation between the third and the seventh centuries. White's provocative discussion of technological change and its impact on social development offers an original approach to medieval history. The journal *Medieval Archaeology,* founded in 1957 and published annually in London contains articles on Britain, often in a wider, European context; each volume also includes notes on current excavations in the British Isles. Another periodical, *Antiquaries Journal,* again published in London, contains papers on medieval topics, including (since 1963) interim reports on the Winchester excavations.

Beckwith, J. *Early medieval art* (London 1964).
Bloch, M. *Feudal society* (English edition London 1960).
Brooke, C. *Europe in the Central Middle Ages, 962–1154* (London 1964).
Brown, P. *The World of late antiquity* (London 1971).
Conant, K. J. *Carolingian and Romanesque architecture* (London 1959).
Douglas, D. *The Norman achievement* (London 1969).
Hussey, J. M. *The Byzantine world* (London 1957).
Leff, G. *Medieval thought* (London 1958).
Luzzatto, G. *An economic history of Italy* (London 1961).
Thompson, M. W. *Novgorod the Great* (London 1967).
White, L. *Medieval technology and social change* (Oxford 1962).
Wilson, D. *The Vikings and their origins* (London 1970).

Glossary

agora: the civic and commercial centre of a Greek city

ashlar: masonry or squared stones laid in regular courses

barrow: mound of earth or stones erected over a burial

basalt: a hard black igneous rock, a volcanic lava

basilica: the town hall of a Roman city situated on one side of the forum; also refers to other buildings (such as churches) with nave, aisles and clerestory lighting

blade: a flake more than twice as long as it is wide. Some workers prefer a more complex definition

canine: the pointed teeth between the incisors and the molars

cire perdue: literally 'lost wax'; a technique of casting metal in which a clay mould is formed round a wax replica of the object to be made. The wax is removed by heating and molten metal poured into the resulting cavity

civitas: a self-governing community in the western part of the Roman Empire, generally co-terminous with the territory of a pre-Roman tribe. Although the civitas capital ranked below the *municipium* and *colonia* in status, it had all the regular features of a Roman city such as forum, basilica and baths. Apart from Verulamium *(municipium)*, London (status uncertain), Colchester, Lincoln, Gloucester, York *(colonia)*, all the cities of Roman Britain were attributed to *civitates*

colonia: originally a settlement of Roman citizens (especially retired legionaries) in potentially hostile territory. From the early second century they were only distinguishable from *municipia* by virtue of their higher status in law

demography: the study of population (Greek: *demos*, people)

dendrochronology: a dating technique based on counting the annual growth rings of trees

fresco: a painting executed on plaster before it has dried. Frequently used of any wall-painting regardless of the technique employed

110

forum: the civic and commercial centre of a Roman city

gerontomorphic: having the form normal in old people

halberd: a dagger-like blade mounted at right angles to its shaft like a battle axe

Iberia: Spain and Portugal

iconoclasm: the Byzantine religious movement which condemned the use of images as idolatry. The movement was sanctioned by the Emperor Leo III in 726 and lasted until 843

hominid: member of the biological family of man (as opposed to apes etc.)

L.B.K.: an abbreviation of the German *Linienbandkeramik* (linear pottery): the name given to a culture

limonite: naturally occurring iron oxide used to make red ochre

lithic: made of stone (Greek: *lithos,* stone)

loess: a type of soil made up of wind-blown rock dust deposited in arid conditions, for instance during the Ice Ages

megalith: a structure, usually a tomb or a temple, built of large stones

municipium: a self-governing community to whom a grant of Roman or Latin citizenship has been made

numismatics: the study of coins (Latin: *nummus,* coin)

oppidum: Latin, a town: here meaning a fortified settlement with earthwork defences

paedomorphic: having the form normal in young children

Palaeolithic: the old stone age: the earliest phase of human prehistory

Pleistocene: the geological period in which the Ice Ages occurred

samian: red-gloss pottery once thought to have been made in Samos, Greece; now known to be the product of factories in Roman Gaul and elsewhere

scriptorium: a room in a monastery devoted to the copying and illumination of manuscripts

stratigraphy: the pattern of successive layers (strata) of earth revealed in an excavation

T.R.B.: an abbreviation of the German *Trichterbecher* (funnel-neck beaker): name given to a culture

tell: a mound formed from the accumulation of collapsed mud-brick buildings over a long period of time

torque: a neck-ring very often of gold. Closely associated with the Celts but also worn by other peoples in antiquity

Index

domestication of plants (*cont.*)
let, 30; oats, 30; olive, 45; rye, 30; spelt wheat, 30; vine, 45

Egyptian civilisation, 38, 39, 40, 58
eoliths, 9–10
Etruscan civilisation, 53, 81

farming: origins of, 23, 27–30, 32; spread of, 30–6
feudalism, 101, 104
fire, use of, 7, 12, 13–14, 25, 26
Flandrian (Mesolithic), 23–5, 35

glaciations, 8–9, 10; sequence of, 9, 10
Globular amphorae culture (Copper Age), 46
Greek civilisation (classical), 52, 53, 56, 58–9, 81

Haçilar (Turkey), 28, 29
Hallstatt culture (Iron Age), 53
hillforts, 51–2, 53, 54
Hittite empire, 50, 52
Homo erectus, 2, 3, 5–8
Homo habilis, 3
houses and dwellings, 4, 12, 25, 30, 34, 35, 62, 66, 87, 88, 95, 103; *see also* architecture, cave dwelling
Horsham culture (Flandrian), 25
hunting and gathering, 3–5, 7, 11, 16, 23, 25, 28, 30–1

Impressed Ware cultures (Neolithic), 33–4
Indus civilisation, 38, 39, 40
inscriptions, 67, 71, 99
interglacials, 8–9
irrigation, 38, 39

Jericho, 28, 29
jewellery and ornaments, 43, 44, 48, 53, 71, 72, 86–7; mirrors, 69; torques, 48

Kurgan culture (Copper Age), 46

L.B.K. culture (Neolithic), 34, 35
la Ferrassie (S. France), 14, 16, 20
La Tène culture (Iron Age), 54
Lascaux (S. France), 20, 21
Lengyel culture (Neolithic), 35
Leptolithic (Upper Palaeolithic) industries, 16–23

Magdalenian industry (Leptolithic), 8, 18, 20, 21, 23, 24
Maglemosian culture (Flandrian), 25
Marcus Aurelius, 58, 62–3
Marseilles, 53, 58, 65, 74
Mauer jaw, 11
megaliths, 36–8, 47
Mesolithic, *see* Flandrian
Mesopotamian civilisation, 38, 39, 40
metal artefact types, 50, 51, 52; agricultural implements, 52, 70; axe-adzes, 43; axes, 43, 44, 45, 48; daggers, 43, 44, 48; halberds, 44, 45, 48; mirrors, 69; spearheads, 43; woodworking tools, 51
metallurgy: bronze metallurgy, 42–5, 48–51; copper metallurgy, 42–5, 46–8; invention of, 38, 39, 42–5; iron metallurgy, 52–4
microliths, 23, 24
Migration Period (Dark Ages), 81, 83–7, 91, 101
mining, 104; of copper, 50; of flint, 35; of silver, 64, 104
Minoan–Mycenaean civilisation, 41, 45–6, 50
missionaries to Britain, 90
Mousterian industry (Middle Palaeolithic), 8, 14, 16
musical instruments in Leptolithic, 22

Natufian culture (Flandrian), 28
Neanderthal man, 3, 11–12, 14–16
'Neolithic Revolution', 23, 27
neoteny, 15

115